A STRAIGHTFORWARD GUIDE
TO
BUSINESS LAW

Robert Franks

www.straightforwardco.co.uk

Straightforward Guides

© Straightforward Publishing 2014

British Cataloguing in Publication data. A catalogue record is available for this book from the British Library.

ISBN

978-1-84716-431-5

Printed in the United Kingdom by Grsovenor Press London

Cover Design by Bookworks Islington

CONTENTS

Introduction

Ch.1 BUSINESS LAW-THE LAW OF CONTRACT-GENERAL   7

1.2 Consideration and contracts   25

1.3 Terms of contract   33

1.4. Errors and contracts   39

1.5 Contracts and illegality   45

1.6 Duress and undue influence   53

1.7 Discharge of a contract   59

1.8 Remedies for breach of contract   67

Ch.2 BUSINESS LAW-NEGLIGENCE AND DUTY OF CARE-GENERAL   73

2. 2 Negligence-causation and remoteness of damage   87

2.3.Negligence-employers liability   99

2.4.Negligence-liability for dangerous or defective products   113

Ch.3. BUSINESS LAW-EMPLOYMENT LAW   119
        EMPLOYMENT CONTRACTS

3.2 Terminating employment   145

3.3 Discrimination in the workplace   159

Ch.4. BUSINESS LAW-COMPANY LAW-GENERAL   167

4.2 The constitution of a company   177

4.3. Company finance   187

Ch.5. BUSINESS LAW-INTELLECTUAL PROPERTY- 205
        PATENTS

5.2.Trade marks   213

5.3.Copyright   225

5.4. Infringement of copyright   235

5.5. Design law   241

Index

Introduction

This first edition of a Straightforward Guide to Business Law is a wide ranging introduction to the law and practice as it affects and influences the environment that regulates business in the United Kingdom.

The book is intended for both the student and layperson and will also be suitable for the professional. Each chapter has relevant case law throughout which provides a suitable back drop to the subject matter.

The book begins with contract law, covering consideration and contracts, terms of contract, errors and contracts, contracts and illegality, duress and undue influence, discharge of a contract and remedies for breach of contract.

Negligence and duty of care is then discussed, covering causation, the liability of the employer and liability for dangerous products. Remedies for negligence are also covered.

Employment law is covered, covering a general outline of law plus discrimination and termination of employment. In addition, company law is covered in depth.

Finally, we discuss the all important area of intellectual property. Patents, trade marks, copyright, infringement of copyright plus design law are covered,

All of the main areas that relate to business law in the United Kingdom are covered in depth. the book should prove ideal to all of those who wish to enhance their knowledge of this important area.

Contracts and advertisements

A distinction is generally made between advertisements for unilateral contracts and advertisements for bilateral contracts. Advertisements for unilateral contracts will include those such as described in the case of Carlill and Carbolic Smokeball Co or those offering a reward for information or for lost property. They are usually treated as offers on the basis that no further negotiations are needed between the parties to the offer and the person making the offer will usually be bound by it. One case is that of Bowerman v Association of British Travel Agents Ltd (1996) in which a school had booked a skiing holiday with a travel agent, which was a member of ABTA.

In this case the tour operator became insolvent and all holidays were cancelled. The school was refunded the money paid for the holiday but not the cost of the travel insurance taken out, which was significant. The case was taken to court and ABTA lost because the notice constituted an offer which the school accepted by contracting with the ABTA member.

Bilateral contracts

Bilateral contracts are the types that advertise specified goods at a certain price such as those found in shop windows and in magazines. They are usually considered invitations to treat on the grounds that they may lead to further bargaining. One such case that highlights this is Partridge v Crittendon (1968). An advertisement in a magazine stated 'Bramblefinch cocks and hens 25shillings each'. As the Bramblefinch was a protected species, the person who placed the advert was charged with unlawfully offering for sale a wild bird which was against the Protection of Birds Act 1954, but the conviction was quashed on the grounds that the advertisement was not an offer but an invitation to treat.

Communication of offers

A valid offer must be communicated to the offeree. It would be unfair for a person to be bound by an offer of which he had no knowledge. This is reflected in Taylor v Laird 1856. The offeree must have clear knowledge of the existence of an offer for it to be enforceable. This is reflected in Inland

Revenue Commissioners v Fry 2001.

An offer can be made to one individual or to the whole world, when the offer can be accepted by any party who had genuine notice of it. In addition, the terms of the contract must be certain. The parties must know in advance what they are contracting over, so any vague words may invalidate the agreement. this is reflected in Guthing v Lynn 1831.

The length of time an offer should last

An offer may cease to exist in any of the following circumstances:

-Where an offeror states that an offer will be open for a specified time

-Where the offeror has not specified how long the offer will remain open, the offer will lapse after a reasonable length of time has passed. How much time can be deemed reasonable will depend on whether the offer was communicated quickly and also on the subject matter.

Some offers are made subject to certain specified conditions, and if these conditions are not in place, the offer may lapse. An offer may lapse if and when the offeree rejects it. For example, if A offers to sell B a car on Tuesday, and B says no, B cannot come back on Wednesday and insist on accepting the offer

A counter offer can terminate the original offer. One case that highlights this is Hyde v Wrench (1840) where the defendant offered to sell his farm for £1000 and the plaintiff responded by offering to buy it at £950-this is termed making a counter offer. The farm owner refused to sell at that price and when the plaintiff later tried to buy the farm at £1000, the original asking price, it was held that this offer was no longer available. The counter offer had terminated the original offer

The death of the offeror can affect the offer. If the offeree knows of the death of the offeror then the offer is terminated. If they did not, the offer still stands, although this is one area of law that is still unclear. It very much depends on the circumstances at the time. An offer may be revoked, withdrawn, at any time until it has been accepted. This is the basic rule, although there are a number of other principles. It is not enough for an offeror simply to change his or her mind about an offer. The offeror must notify the offeree that the offer has been revoked. Revocation does not specifically have to be communicated by the offeror, it can be by another reliable party.

Acceptance of an offer

Acceptance of an offer must be unconditional, accepting the precise terms of the offer. Where the process of negotiation is long and difficult, it might be difficult to pinpoint exactly when an offer has been made and accepted. In such cases a court will examine the precise course of negotiations to ascertain whether the parties have reached agreement, if at all and when. This process can be complicated when the so-called 'battle of forms' occurs. Rather than negotiating terms each time a contract is made many companies try to use standard conditions, which will be printed on headed stationary, such as order forms and delivery notes. The 'battle of forms' occurs when one party sends a form stating that the contract is on their terms, and the other party responds by sending back the forms and stating that the contract is on their terms. The general rule in these cases is that the 'last shot' wins the battle. Each new form issued is treated as a counter offer, so that when one party performs its obligation under the contract the action will be seen as acceptance by the other side. One simple case that illustrates this is British Road Services v Crutchley (Arthur V) Ltd (1968). The plaintiffs delivered some whisky to the defendants for storage. The BRS driver handed the defendants a delivery note, which listed the company's terms of carriage. The note was accepted and stamped with Crutchley's terms and conditions and the court held that by accepting this, the BRS driver had accepted a counter offer. Although many cases are simple, other more recent case law has held that the last shot will not always succeed.

It is a basic assumption that there is no acceptance until the act has been thoroughly performed. However, in some cases, part performance may amount to acceptance. In Errington v Errington (1952) a father bought a house in his own name for £750, borrowing £500 of the price from a building society. He bought the house for his son and daughter in law to live in, and told them that they must meet the mortgage repayments. If they met the payments the house would be signed over to them on completion of the term. The couple moved in and began to pay the mortgage, but they never in fact made the promise to continue with the payments until the mortgage was paid off, which meant that the contract was unilateral.

When the father later died, the people in charge of his affairs sought to withdraw the offer. The Court of Appeal held that it was too late to do this. The part performance of the son and daughter in law constituted an acceptance of the contract and the father and his representatives after death were bound by the resulting contract unless the son and daughter in law ceased the payments, in which case the offer was no longer binding.

A request for information about an offer does not constitute a counter offer, so the original offer remains open. If an offeree has to accept an offer in a specified manner, then only acceptance by that method or an equally effective one will be binding

Communicating acceptance of an offer

An acceptance will not usually take effect until it is clearly communicated to the offeror. However, there are some circumstances where acceptance may take effect without it being communicated to the offeror. An offer may clearly state, or indeed imply, that acceptance need not be communicated to the offeror. An offeror who fails to receive an acceptance through their own fault may be prevented from claiming that the non-communication means they should not be bound by the contract.

The general rule for acceptances by post is that they take effect when they are posted, rather than when they are communicated. The postal rule was laid down in the case of Adams v Lindsell (1818), when on the 2nd of September 1817, the defendants wrote to the plaintiffs, who were in the wool processing business, offering to sell them a quantity of sheep fleeces, and stating that they required an answer 'in course of post'. However, the defendants did not address the letter correctly and it did not reach the plaintiffs until the evening of September the 5th. The plaintiffs posted their acceptance the same evening, and it reached the defendants on the 9th of September. If the original letter had been correctly addressed it would have reached the plaintiffs by the 7th of September. Because it was incorrectly addressed it did not and no reply was received and the wool was sold to a third party. The issue was whether a sale had been made before the sale of the wool to the third party. The court heard that the contract was concluded as soon as the acceptance was posted and that the defendants were bound from the evening of 5th September so should not have sold the wool to a third party.

There are certain exceptions to the postal rule. The offeror may avoid the postal rule by making it a specific term of their offer that acceptance will only take effect when it is communicated to them.

The postal rule has limited application to modern communications technology. In Entores Ltd v Miles Far East Corp, offer and acceptance communicated by telex were valid because the method was so instantaneous that the parties were deemed to be dealing as if face-to-face, even though they were in different countries. The time when these forms of communication are used may cause problems in determining if a contract is made, as when a fax is sent out of office hours. Now offer and acceptance in the case of electronic communication is governed by the Consumer Protection (Distance Selling) Regulations 2000. This gives the buyer the right to be informed of the right to cancel within seven days, description, price, arrangements for payment and identity of seller, and to be given written confirmation, without which a contract is not formed. Under EU Electronic Commerce Directive 2000/31 no contract can be made electronically until the buyer has received acknowledgement of his acceptance. the Directive has been implemented through the Electronic Commerce (EC Directive) Regulations 2000.

Ignorance of the offer

It is generally accepted that a person cannot accept an offer of which they are unaware, because in order to create a binding contract, the parties must reach agreement. This is a very important principle.

Tenders, auctions and the sale of land

The rules outlined above also apply to the sale of land and to sales by tender and auction. If a large organization, such as a company or government department needs to contract a supplier of goods or services, it will, more often than not, advertise for tenders, i.e., bids. Organizations wishing to supply goods or services will reply, detailing price for these services. The advertiser will choose from the replies and contact the successful tender. As a general rule, the request for tenders is regarded as an invitation to treat, (see previous) so there is no specific obligation to accept any of the tenders sent. The tenders themselves are offers and a contract does not come into existence until one is accepted. However, where a party has issued an invitation to tender, it is bound to consider all correctly submitted tenders. One such case highlighting this is Blackpool and Fylde Aero Club v Blackpool Borough Council (1990). Blackpool BC invited tenders from people who were interested in operating leisure flights from the local airfield. Tenders had to be submitted to the town hall by a stated deadline. The Aero Club submitted its application on time but the council refused to consider it, as due to an error on their part, they mistakenly believed that the tender had been submitted after the deadline.

It was held that the council's invitation to tender was a unilateral offer to consider all tenders which fell within its rules. The tender constituted an offer which had been accepted by the Aero Club. The offer was accepted by any party who put in a tender. Thus the council were obliged to consider all tenders (acceptances) to their offer, including the Aero Club tender. They were not, of course, obliged to accept the tender.

In some cases however, an invitation for tenders may in itself be an offer. The main example of this is where the invitation to tender makes it clear that the lowest tender (or highest) will be accepted. The implications of choosing to accept a tender depend on what sort of tender is involved.

Specific tenders

Where an invitation to tender specifies that a particular quantity of goods is required on a particular date, or between certain dates, agreeing to one of the tenders submitted will constitute acceptance of an offer, creating a contract between the parties.

Non-specific tenders

Some invitations to tender are not specific, and may for example simply state that certain goods may be required, up to a particular maximum quantity, with deliveries to be made if and when requested. For example, an invitation to tender made by a hospital may ask for tenders to supply goods, if and when required. In this case, taking up one of the tenders submitted does not amount to acceptance of an offer in the contractual sense and there is no contract. The hospital may take the goods all at once, some at a time or none at all. It is not bound.

Auction sales

The parties to an auction sale are the bidder and the owner of the goods. The auctioneer supplies a service and is not party to the contract between buyer and seller.

Sale of land

The standard rules of contract apply to the sale of land, including buildings. However, the court applies the rules strictly in the case of land, tending to require very clear evidence of an intention to be bound before they will state that an offer has been made.

In Harvey v Facey (1893) the plaintiffs sent the defendants a telegram asking 'will you sell us Bumper Hall Pen? Telegraph lowest cash price'. The reply arrived back stating 'Lowest price for Bumper Hall pen £900'. The plaintiffs then sent a telegram saying 'we agree to buy Bumper Hall Pen for £900. Please send us your title deeds'. On these facts, the Privy Council held that there was no contract. They regarded the telegram from the defendants as a statement of price only. It was therefore not an offer which could be accepted by the third telegram.

In practice there are rigid procedures involved in the sale of land. The first is the 'sale subject to contract', where the parties agree to the sale and the implication is that there is a good deal of proving and other work before a contract is in existence. The next stage is the exchange of contract, where the buyer and seller agree to the terms of the formal contract. Once the contracts are exchanged then the contract is binding and any backing out can result in a claim for damages and lost deposit.

Certainty of contract

In order to be viewed as a binding contract, an agreement must be absolutely certain. That is, it should not be vague or incomplete. One such case that amplifies this is that of Scammell v Ouston (1941) where the parties agreed that Ouston could buy a van from Scammell, giving his lorry in part exchange paying the balance over two-years on hire purchase terms. Scammell decided to back out and claimed that there was no contract between the parties.

The House of Lords agreed, pointing out that the courts would uphold an agreement if there really was one, in this case the terms were too vague, particularly the agreement to pay on Hire Purchase Terms.

In certain cases, parties may leave details vague, particularly when dealing with fluctuating prices and other factors. Provisions should be in the contract stating how they should be clarified.

Terms implied into contract by statute

In some cases, statute will override contract and will provide that certain provisions should be read into contracts even though they have not been specifically agreed between the parties. For example, under the Sale of Goods act 1979, an agreement for the sale of goods can become binding as soon as the parties have agreed to buy and sell, with the details of the contract being laid down by law, or determined by the standard of reasonableness. In such a case, the parties do not even have had to agree on a price. The buyer is entitled to pay a reasonable price. Terms implied by statute will be examined further on in this book.

Intention to create legal relations

One major principle of contract law is that of intention to create legal relations. If two or more parties make an agreement without the intention of being legally bound by it, the agreement will not be regarded as a contract.

As far as intent to be legally bound is concerned, contracts can be divided into domestic and social agreements on one hand, and commercial agreements on the other. Where the agreement falls into the former category there is an assumption that the parties do not intend to create legal relations. The reverse is true when it comes to commercial agreements.

Domestic and social agreements

Where a husband and wife who are living together as one household make an agreement, the courts will assume that they do not intend to be legally bound, unless the agreement states other wise. In Balfour v Balfour (1919) the defendant was a civil servant stationed in Sri Lanka. Whilst the couple were on leave in England, Mrs. Balfour was taken ill, and it became clear that her husband would have to return by himself. He promised to pay her maintenance of £30 per month. They eventually separated and the husband refused to make any more payments. The Court of Appeal decided he was not bound to make further payments, as when the agreement was made there was no intention to create legal relations. Likewise, agreements between parents and children are assumed not to be legally binding.

Social agreements

The presumption that an agreement is not intended to be legally binding is also applied to social relationships between people who are not related. With both the above though, there can be exceptions.

Commercial agreements

There is a strong presumption in commercial agreements that the parties intend to be legally bound, and unless clear words are used this presumption stands. Where the words of a business agreement are ambiguous, the courts will favor the interpretation that suggests that the parties did intend to create legal relations.

The capacity to enter into a contract

There are categories of people in society whose power to make contracts is limited by law. The main categories are minors and people considered incapable of contracting due to mental disorders or some other condition of incapacity such as drunkenness or under influence of certain drugs. In addition, the contracting capacity of a company or corporation will also have a bearing, i.e. the legal capacity to enter into a contract in the first place. The basic common law rule is that contracts do not bind minors. In some cases however, as in much of contract law, there are contracts that will bind minors. The main contracts binding on a minor are contracts to supply 'necessaries'. Under the Sale of Goods Act 1979, necessaries means 'goods suitable to the condition in life of the minor or other person concerned and to his actual requirements at the time of sale and delivery'. When deciding if a contract is one for necessaries, the courts first of all determine whether the goods or services are capable of amounting to necessaries in law, and then consider whether they are necessary for the minor in question. Two cases highlight this point. In Nash v Inman (1908) a student purchased 11 silk waistcoats while still a minor. He argued that they comprised 'goods suitable to his condition in life, and to his actual requirements at the time of sale and delivery'. It was held that the silk waistcoats were suitable to the conditions of life of a Cambridge undergraduate at that time, but they were not suitable to his actual needs as he already had a sufficient supply of waistcoats.

A more recent case was that of Proform Sports Management Limited v Proactive Sports management Limited and Another (2006). In this case, footballer Wayne Rooney signed a two year management and agency agreement with the claimant when he was aged 15. Rooney later terminated the contract. It was held that the agreement was not a contract of apprenticeship, education or service substantially to the footballer's benefit thus he was entitled to avoid it.

Mental incapacity

This category covers people who suffer from mental disability, and those who are drunk when the contract is made. In general terms, contracts made with people in either state will be valid unless, very importantly, at the time the contract was made, the person is incapable of understanding the nature of the transaction and the other party knows this. In such circumstances, the contract is voidable. The party suffering the disability can choose to void it.

Where one party is incapable, through disability as described, of understanding the nature of the contract, but the other party is unaware, the courts will ignore the disability. One important case highlighting this is Hart v O'Connor (1985) the Privy Council held that a person of unsound mind was bound by his agreement to sell some land because when the contract was made the buyer did not realize that the buyer had any mental incapacity. The fact also that language may be a barrier does not render a person incapable of making a contract.

Corporations

A corporation is a legal entity that is treated by law as having a separate identity from the persons who constitute it. There are three main types of corporation: registered companies, corporations established by statute and chartered corporations. Each has a different level of contracting ability.

Registered companies

These are companies registered under the Companies Act 1985 (as amended) most commercial companies. When registering, companies must supply a document that regulates their activities called a memorandum of association, which contains information including an objects clause, laying down the range of activities that their company can engage in. Under the 1989 Act a company can be liable for a contract made outside its stated activities if the other party has acted in good faith.

Statutory companies

These corporations are created by an Act of Parliament, for specific purposes, the Independent Broadcasting Authority is an example, as are local authorities. The statute creating the particular corporation will specify the purposes for which that corporation may make contracts. Any contracted outside of these purposes is null and void.

Chartered corporations

These are corporations set up by Royal Charter, which means that their rights are officially granted by the Crown. Examples are charities and some universities and other educational institutions. They have the same contractual capacity as an adult human being.

Formalities

We have discussed the fact that an agreement does not have to take a specific written form in order to be deemed a binding contract. A contract can be oral. One famous recent case involving an oral contract was Hadley v Kemp (1990) where Gary Kemp was the songwriter in the group Spandau Ballet. He was sued by other members of then group for royalties received for the group's music. The basis of the claim was that there was an oral agreement to share royalties. They were unable to prove the existence of any oral agreement and their claim failed.

Contracts which must be made by deed

The Law of Property Act 1925 states that a contract for a lease of more than three years must be made by deed, which basically means that it must be put into a formal document, signed in front of witnesses.

Contracts which must be in writing

Some statutes lay down that certain types of contract must be in writing. Most contracts involving sales of land must be in writing, under the Law of Property Act 1989. Other contracts that need to be in writing are those involving the transfers of shares in a limited company (Companies Act 1985 (as amended), bills of exchange; cheques and promissory notes (Bills of Exchange Act (1882); and regulated consumer credit agreements, such as hire purchase agreements (Consumer Credit Act 1974).

Contracts which must be evidenced in writing

Contracts of guarantee (where one party guarantees the obligations of another, such as parents guaranteeing a sons or daughters overdraft) are required to be 'evidenced in writing'. Contracts for sale or disposition of land before 27th September 1989 are still covered by the old law prior to the Law of Property Act 1989. Evidenced in writing means that although the contract itself may not be a written one, there must be written evidence of the transaction. The evidence must have existed before one party tried to enforce the contract against the other, and it must be signed by the party against whom the contract is to be enforced.

****

1.2

CONSIDERATION AND CONTRACTS

As we have seen, English law states that a contract is not usually binding unless it is supported by consideration. Consideration is usually said to mean that each party to a contract must give something in return for what is gained from the other party. Very basically, if there is a dispute and you wish to enforce someone's promise to you must prove that you gave something in return for that promise.

Consideration may be goods or services, a thing or a service. Many problems concerning consideration arise not when a contract is made but when one or other of the parties to the contract seeks to modify it, such as paying a lower price than agreed or supplying a different good or service.

Promisor and Promisee

In most contracts, it is the case that two promises will be exchanged, so each party to the contract is promisor and promisee. In a contract case, the claimant will often be arguing that the defendant has broken the promise made to the claimant and therefore the claimant will usually be the promisee. One example is if A contracts to build a conservatory and B promises to pay £5000 for the conservatory, there are two promises in this contract. A's promise to build a conservatory and B's promise to pay. If A fails to build the conservatory B can sue him. If the issue of consideration arises, B will seek to prove that his promise to pay £5000 was consideration for A's promise for building the conservatory. In that action, A will be the promisor and B the promisee. However, reverse the situation and B fails to pay, then A will sue and, if consideration is at issue, A will have to prove that his promise to build the conservatory was consideration for B's promise to pay. In that action, A will be the promisee and B the promisor.

'Executory' and 'executed' consideration

Consideration can fall into two categories: executory and executed. Executed consideration is the performance of an act in return for a promise. Executory consideration is when the defendant makes a promise, and the plaintiff offers a counter promise – you promise to deliver goods to me and I promise to pay for them when they arrive, the promise is executory because it is something to be done in the future.

Consideration must be given in return for the promise or act of the other party. Something done, given, or promised beforehand will not be counted as consideration. A classic case concerning this arose in Roscorla v Thomas (1842). The defendant sold the plaintiff a horse. After the sale was completed, the defendant told the plaintiff that the animal was 'sound and free from any vice'. This was not the actual truth and the plaintiff sued. The court held that the defendants promise was unenforceable, because it was made after the sale. If the promise about the horse's condition had been made before, the plaintiff would have provided consideration for it by buying the horse. As it was made after the sale, the consideration was past, for it had not been given in return for the promise.

There are two exceptions to the rule that past consideration is no consideration. The first is where the past consideration was provided at the promisors request, and it was understood that payment would be made. The second is the bill of exchange. Under s27 of the Bills of Exchange Act 1882, an antecedent debt or 'liability' may be consideration for receipt of a bill of exchange.

The rules of consideration-Consideration need not be adequate

The law of contract regulates the making of bargains. As freedom of contract is vital, the law is not concerned with whether a party has made a good bargain or a bad one. Adequacy is given its normal meaning-the contract is enforceable even if the price does not match the value of what is being gained under the agreement. One such case that reflects this is Thomas v Thomas (1842). before he died Thomas expressed a wish that his wife should be allowed to remain in his house although there was no mention of this in his will. The executors carried out his wish but charged the widow a nominal ground rent of £1 a year. When they later tried to dispossess her they failed.

Consideration must be sufficient

Consideration offered is sufficient provided that:

- It is real (White v Bluett (1853)
- It is tangible (Ward v Byham (1956)
- It has some discernible value (Chappel v Nestle (1960); and
- Economic value is measured against benefit gained.

Consideration must not be past

Consideration must follow rather than precede agreement. This prevents coercion by suppliers of goods and services.

Consideration must be of economic value

What this principle basically means is that there must be some physical value, rather than just an emotional or sentimental value.

Consideration can be a promise not to sue

If one party has a possible civil claim against the other, a promise not to enforce that claim is good consideration for a promise given in return. One clear example is if A crashes into B's car then A can promise not to sue if B pays for the damage.

Performance of an existing duty

Where a promisee already owes the promisor a legal duty, then in theory performing that duty should not in itself be consideration. If the promisee does nothing more than they are already obliged to do, they are suffering no detriment and the promisor is only getting a benefit to which he or she is entitled. Existing duties can be divided into three categories: public duties; contractual duties to the promisor; and contractual duties to a third party.

Existing public duty

Where a person is merely carrying out duties they are legally bound to perform – such as police officer or juror, doing that alone will not be consideration. However, where a promisee is under a public duty, but does something beyond the call of that duty, that extra act amounts to consideration. In Glasbrook Brothers v Glamorgan County Council (1925) the owners of a South Wales Mine asked the police to place a guard at their colliery during a strike. The police suggested that regular checks by mobile patrol would be adequate but the owners replied that they wanted something more intensive and the police agreed at an extra cost of £2,200. After the strike the owners refused to pay saying that the police had a duty to protect their property. The courts held in favor of the police saying that the police did not have a duty to supply the cover they did, only the cover they deemed sufficient. Anything over and above was deemed consideration.

Existing contractual duty to the promisor

The position on contractual duties and consideration has changed from the traditional position whereby the performance of an existing contractual duty owed to a promisor was not consideration. In Stilk v Myrick (1809) two sailors deserted a ship during a voyage and the captain was unable to find replacements. The remaining crew-members were promised extra wages for sailing the ship back to London but the captain refused to pay on arrival and the sailors sued with the court holding that there was no consideration as the sailors had already contracted to sail the boat back to its destination. In Hartley v Ponsonby (1857) half the crew deserted and the remaining crew were offered extra wages to carry on the journey. At the end the captain refused to pay and the crew sued and won, as the courts held that there was consideration as the crew were to small to sail the boat adequately and extra money was justified.

An exception to the rule that performance of an existing contractual obligation owed to the promisor will not amount to consideration will occur where a party can be seen to receive an extra benefit from the other party's agreement to carry out his existing obligations. One such case that highlights this is that of Williams v Roffey Brothers (1991). In this case the defendants (the main contractors) were refurbishing a block of flats. They sub-contracted the carpentry works to the plaintiff. The plaintiff ran into financial difficulties, whereupon the defendants agreed to pay the plaintiff an additional sum if they completed the work on time. It was held that where a party to an existing contract later agrees to pay an 'extra bonus' in order that the other party performs his obligations under the original contract, then the new agreement is binding if the party agreeing to pay the bonus has thereby obtained some new practical advantage or avoided a disadvantage. In this particular case, the advantage was the avoidance of a penalty clause and the expense of finding new carpenters, among other factors.

Existing contractual duty to a third party

In some cases two parties make a contract to provide a benefit to a third party. If one of the parties (A) makes a further promise to that third party to provide the benefit they have already contracted to provide, that further promise can be good consideration for a promise made by the third party in return-even though nothing more than the contractual duty is being promised by A.

One case that illustrates this is Scotson v Pegg (1861). Scotson contracted to supply a cargo of coal to a third party, X, or to anyone X nominated. Scotson was instructed by X to deliver the coal to Pegg, and Pegg promised to unload the coal at a stated rate of pay. He subsequently failed to do the agreed unloading. Scotson sued Pegg, claiming that their promise to deliver coal to him was consideration for his promise to unload it. Pegg claimed that this could not be consideration, since Scotson was already bound to supply the coal under the contract with X. The court upheld Scotson's claim: delivery of the coal was consideration because it was a benefit to Pegg, and a detriment to Scotson in that it prevented them from having the option of breaking their contract with X.

Waiver and Promissory estoppel

These are ways of making some kind of promise binding even where there is no consideration. Waiver has traditionally applied where one party agrees not to enforce their strict rights under the contract by, for example, accepting delivery later than agreed. One case that illustrates the doctrine of waiver is that of Hickman v Haynes (1875). A buyer asked the seller to deliver goods later than originally agreed and then when the delivery was made refused to accept it. The seller sued for breach of contract, the buyer responded by arguing that the seller was in breach, for delivering later than specified. The courts rejected the buyer's argument on the ground s that the delivery was made at the buyer's request.

Promissory estoppel (stopping the contract on the basis of a promise) is a newer doctrine than waiver, developing the concept. It was introduced by Lord Denning in the Central London Property Trust Ltd v High Trees (1947) where owners of a block of flats had promised to accept reduced rents in 1939. There was no consideration for their promise but Lord Denning nevertheless stated that he would estop them from recovering any arrears. He based his case on the decision in Hughes v Metropolitan Railways (1875). In this case, under the lease the tenants were obliged to keep the premises in good repair, and in October 1874, the landlord gave them six months notice to do some repairs stating that if they were not done in time, the lease would be forfeited. In November the two parties began to negotiate the possibility of the tenants buying the lease, the tenants stating in the meantime that they would not carry out the repairs. By December the negotiations had broken down and at the end of the six-month notice period, the landlord claimed that the lease was forfeited because the tenants had not done the repairs. The House of Lords (now Supreme Court) held however, that the landlord's conduct was an implied promise to the tenants that he would not enforce the forfeiture at the end of the notice period, and in not doing the repairs, the tenants had been relying on this premise. It was seen that the six-month notice period began again when negotiations broke down.

The exact scope of the doctrine is a matter of debate, but certain requirements must be met:

- Estoppel only applies to the modification of discharge of an existing contractual obligation. It cannot create a new contract.
- It can only be used as a 'shield' and not a 'sword'.

- The promise not to enforce rights must be clear and unequivocal.
- It must be inequitable for the promisor to go back on his promise.
- The promisee must have acted in reliance on the promise, although not necessarily to his detriment.

Agreement by deed

There is one other way in which a promise can be made binding without consideration: it can be put into a document called a deed. An agreement by deed is often described as a 'formal' contract. Other types of contract are known as simple contracts. The procedure for making a contract by deed is laid down in s.1 of the Law of Property (Miscellaneous Provisions) Act 1989 and usually involves signing a formal document in the presence of a witness. Deeds are usually used to give legal effect to what otherwise might be a gratuitous gift, which could be unenforceable for lack of consideration.

•••••••••••••••••

1.3

TERMS OF CONTRACT

Once a contract has been formed, it is necessary to define the scope of the obligations which each party incurs. Terms of contracts describe the respective duties and obligations of each party to the contract. As well as the contractual terms laid out and agreed by parties to a contract, called express terms, there may also be implied terms – terms that are 'read into' a contract because of the facts of the agreement and the apparent intention of the parties or the law on specific types of contract.

Oral statements

In all transactions, with the exception of the simplest, there will be some negotiations before a contract is made. These are usually oral statements or based on oral statements. Problems can arise following oral statements when parties cannot agree whether the statement was intended to be binding. In considering questions such as these a court will classify statements made during negotiations as either representations or terms. A representation is a statement that may have encouraged one of the parties to make the contract, but is not itself part of the contract, while a term is an undertaking that is part of the contract.

Representation can also be construed as misrepresentation, which is a common cause of dispute. Whether a statement is either a representation or a term is mainly a question of the party's intentions. If the parties have indicated that a particular statement is a term of their contract, then the court will carry out that intention.

Written terms of a contract

Written terms can be incorporated into a contract in three different ways: by signature, by reasonable notice and by a previous course of dealing.

The parol evidence rule

Under this rule, where there is a written contract, extrinsic (parole) evidence cannot change the express terms laid down in that document. Extrinsic evidence includes oral statements and written material such as draft contracts or letter, whether relating to pre-contract negotiations or the parties post contractual behavior. One case that illustrates the parole evidence rule is Henderson v Arthur (1907). The plaintiffs and the defendant were parties to a lease that contained a covenant for the payment of rent quarterly in advance, although before the lease was drawn up the parties agreed that the rent could be paid in arrears. When the tenant was sued for not paying quarterly in advance, he pointed out this prior agreement. The court held that the terms of prior oral agreement could not be substituted for the terms of a later formal contract covering the same transaction. There are a few exceptions to the parol evidence rule, the following being the main ones:

Rectification

Where a document is intended to record a previous oral agreement but fails to do that accurately, evidence of the oral agreement will be admitted.

Partially written agreements

Where there is a written agreement, but the parties clearly intended it to be qualified by other written or oral statements, the parol evidence rule is displaced.

Implied terms

The parol evidence rule only applies where a party seeks to use existing evidence to alter the express terms of a contract. Where a contract is of a type that is unusually subject to terms implied by law and statute, parol evidence may be given to support, or to deny, the usual implication.

Collateral agreements

There is a way in which an oral statement can be deemed binding, even though it conflicts with a written contract and does not fall within any of the exceptions to the parol rule. If one party says something like 'I will sign this document if you will assure me that it means….' The courts may find that two contracts have been created, the written agreement and a collateral contract based on the oral statement.

Construction of express terms in contracts

The courts will sometimes have to determine the construction of an express term within a contract. The courts will have to 'seek the meaning which the document would convey to a reasonable person having all the background knowledge which would have reasonably been available to parties at the time of entering into the agreement'. The courts start by presuming that the parties meant what they said. The courts would also look at the outcome of the words and meaning to see if they create an absurdity or are inconsistent with the rest of the contract.

Implied terms

As well as the express terms laid down in the contract, further terms may be sometimes read into the contract by the courts. These implied terms are divided into four groups: terms implied by fact, terms implied by law, terms implied by custom and terms implied by trade usage. Terms implied by fact are terms not laid out in the contract, but which it is assumed both parties would have intended to include if they had thought about it, they may have left them out by mistake. In order to decide what the intention of the parties was, the courts have developed two tests, the 'officious bystander test, and the 'business efficacy' test.

The officious bystander test was laid down in Shirlaw v Southern Foundries (1926). The Judge said, …'that which in any contract is left to be implied and need not be expressed is something so obvious that it goes without saying: so that, if while the parties were making their bargain, an officious bystander were to suggest some express provision for it in the agreement, they would testily suppress him with a common 'oh, of course'. The business efficacy test covers terms which one side alleges must be implied to make the contract work, to give it business efficacy. Terms implied by law are terms which the law dictates must be present in certain types of contract-in some cases whether the parties intended them or not. In Liverpool Council v Irwin (1977) the defendants lived in a council maisonette that was part of a high-rise block in Liverpool. The block was in a bad condition and tenants withheld rent and the case went to court with the tenants arguing that the council was in breach of contract (tenancy). The council argued that there was no agreement to keep the block in good condition and the courts argued that good repair and safety were implied terms of contract. The council lost the case.

Terms implied by custom can be implied into a contract if there is evidence that under local custom they would normally be there.

Terms implied by trade usage would normally be part of a contract made by parties in a particular trade or business.

Misrepresentation in contracts

Even in cases where a contract clearly meets the requirements of offer and acceptance, consideration and intent to create legal relations, it will still not be binding if, at the time the contract was made, certain factors were present which meant that there was no genuine concern. These are known as vitiating factors (because they vitiate, or invalidate, consent). The vitiating factors that the law recognizes as preventing a contract are misrepresentation, mistake, duress, undue influence and illegality. In these cases, the innocent party may set the contract aside if he wishes.

If one party has been induced to enter into a contract by a statement made by the other party, and that statement is untrue, the contract is voidable and the innocent party may also be able to claim damages. For a misrepresentation to be actionable it must be untrue, a statement of fact not opinion, and it must have induced the innocent party to enter into the contract.

There are four different types of misrepresentation, fraudulent misrepresentation, where there is clear deceit, negligent, where misrepresentation arises through acts of negligence but not deceit and innocent misrepresentation which is not fraudulent but is still clear misrepresentation. The effect of a misrepresentation is generally to make a contract voidable, rather than void, so the contract will continue to exist unless or until the injured party chooses to have it set aside by the courts by means of rescission.

Rescission is an equitable remedy that sets the contract aside and puts the parties back in the position where they were before the misrepresentation. An injured party who decides to rescind the contract may do so by notifying the other party or, if this is not possible owing to the conduct of the party, by taking some reasonable action to indicate the intention to default. A case that illustrates this is Car and Universal Finance Co Ltd v Caldwell (1965) where the defendant sold and delivered a car and was paid by cheque. The cheque bounced, by which time the car and buyer had disappeared. The defendant notified the police and the Automobile Association. While the police were investigating the buyer sold the car to a dealer who knew that the car was not the buyer's to sell. Finally, the car dealer sold the car to the claimants who bought it in good faith. The court of Appeal held that by contacting the police and the AA the claimant had made his intention to rescind the contract clear. As soon as this happened the ownership of the car reverted to him. This meant that at the time the car was sold back to the claimant the car was not anyone's to sell.

Another case illustrating this is Whittington v Seale-Hayne (1900) where the plaintiffs, breeders of prize poultry, were induced to take a lease of the defendant's premises by his innocent representation that the premises were in a sanitary condition. Under the lease, the plaintiffs covenanted to execute any works required by any local or public authority. Owing to the insanitary conditions of the premises, the water supply was poisoned, the plaintiff's manager and his family became very ill, and the poultry became valueless for breeding purposes or died. The court rescinded the lease, and held that the plaintiffs could recover an indemnity for what they had spent on rates, rent and repairs under the covenants in the lease, because these expenses arose necessarily out of the contract. It refused to award compensation for other leases, since to do so would be to award damages, not an indemnity, there being no obligation created by the contract to carry on a poultry farm on the premises or to employ a manager, etc.

Representation and terms of a contract

Section 1 of the Misrepresentation Act 1967 provides that where a misrepresentation becomes a term of the contract, the innocent party may bring an action for both misrepresentation and breach of contract. Under section 3 of this Act, as amended by the Unfair Contract Terms Act 1977, exemption clauses that attempt to exclude or limit liability for misrepresentations are operative only if reasonable. This provision is illustrated in Walker v Boyle (1982) where the seller of a house told the buyer that there were no disputes regarding the boundaries of the property. This was not true. This misrepresentation appeared to entitle the buyer to rescind the contract and notwithstanding a clause seeking to deny this, the court granted a rescission.

****

1.4

ERRORS AND CONTRACTS

The general rule is that a mistake has no effect on a contract, but certain mistakes of a fundamental nature, sometimes called operative mistakes can render a contract void at common law.. However, the law in this area operates quite rigidly.

The general principles

There are two types of mistake within contract law, Common mistake and cross-purpose mistake. Both are underpinned by general rules. There is an objective principle, or test that the court will apply when considering mistakes within contracts. The courts do not ask the parties to the contract what they thought they were entering into but rather they consider what an onlooker would have thought it was each party was agreeing to. This is very much akin to the 'officious bystander test' referred to earlier.

Another key principle is that in order to void a contract the mistake must be made before the contract is completed. One case that illustrates this is Amalgamated Investment and Property Co Ltd v John Walker and sons Ltd (1977). In this case, a contract was made for the sale of a warehouse, for £1,710,000. The sellers knew that the purchasers were buying the warehouse with the intention of redeveloping it. The day after the contract was signed, the Department of the Environment, as it was then, made the property a listed building. This made it more difficult for the buyers to get permission to redevelop. Without this permission the warehouse would be worth considerably less. Neither party to the contract had been aware that the DOE were going to list the building.

The Court of Appeal held that the contract was valid as at the time of the agreement both parties were perfectly correct in their belief that the building was not listed, so there was no operative mistake. In the past, only a mistake of fact could negate a contract not a mistake of law. However, in the light of certain key cases, this is not now the case.

Common mistake

Having explored the general principles underpinning the treatment of mistakes in contract it is now time to explore the two types of mistake more thoroughly.

Common mistakes are also known as identical mistakes, shared mistake or mistake nullifying consent. In this situation both parties make the same mistake-for example if A buys an antique from B which both parties think is rare and valuable, such as Wedgwood Pottery, but which is in fact a fake, they have made a shared mistake which would only render the contract void if the mistake relates to one of three subjects which the courts consider fundamental to the contract: the existence of the subject matter, its ownership and, in limited cases, its quality.

A mistake as to the existence of subject matter will usually only concern goods to be sold-if for example A purports to sell a motorbike to B, and it is then discovered that the motorbike has been destroyed by fire, the contract will not be valid. It can apply equally to other subject matter. The main test is, do the goods or other exist at the time of a contract. One case that illustrates this is Scott v Coulson (1993). A life insurance policy was taken out, covering a person's death. In fact the person was already dead so the contract was null and void.

It is not always the case that the non-existence of subject matter will render the contract null and void. There have been several cases that obscure this general principle. One such case was Couturier v Hastie (1856) that involved a contract to buy a cargo of corn, which, at the time the contract was made was supposed to be on a ship sailing to England from the Mediterranean port of Salonica. In fact by that time the corn had already been sold by the master of the ship to a buyer in Tunis because the corn had started to deteriorate and go off. This is a common occurrence and the master's action was the usual accepted solution. For the purposes of the original contract the corn had ceased to exist. The sellers claimed that the buyers still had an obligation to pay as per the contract. The House of Lords held that the buyer did not have to pay for the corn, as the goods did not exist. There was no mistake; quite simply the corn did not exist.

Mistake as to title
Very rarely, a situation will arise in which one party agrees to transfer property to the other but unknown to both party's, the latter already owns that property. In such a case, the contract will be void for mistake. This is obviously very rare but has happened on occasion.

Mistaken identity
There is a presumption that a contract is valid even where one party has made a mistake as to the identity of the other. However, this presumption can be denied or negated by the party who has made the mistake. If this is done the contract is void at common law. In order to achieve this the mistaken party must prove that they intended to deal with a person other than the person who was in fact the other party to the contract, and that the identity of the other party was regarded as of fundamental importance.

One key case that illustrates this is Cundy V Lindsey (1878). The claimants received an order for a large number of handkerchiefs from a Mr Blenkarn of 37 Wood Street, Cheapside. Mr Blenkarn rented a room at that address, and further down the road at 123 Cheapside, were the offices of a firm called Blenkiron and Co. Blenkarn signed his name so it looked liked Blenkiron. The claimants sent off their goods addressed to Blenkiron and Co. Mr Blenkarn received them and by the time that the fraud was discovered he had sold them to the defendants, Cundy, who had bought them in good faith. The claimants sued the defendants to get the money back, and their success in this depended on whether it could be proved that there was a contract between the claimants and Blenkarn.

The House of Lords held that there was no contract between Blenkarn and the claimants, because they had intended all along to deal with Blenkiron and Co. The court very importantly held that 'between him and them there was no consensus of mind which could lead to...any contract whatsoever.

41

Mistake over the terms of the contract

Where one party is mistaken as to the terms of the contract, and the other knows this, the contract will be void, regardless of whether the term is fundamental.

Mistakes relating to documents

Where a mistake relates to a written document there are two special remedies in existence, *non est factum* and rectification.

Although the general principle is that a contract becomes effective when a person signs it, regardless of whether they understood it, *non est factum* (this is not my deed) becomes operative where a person signs a document believing it to be something totally different from what it actually was. This remedy may make the contract void. In order to void the contract the person seeking this remedy must prove three things: that the signature was induced by a trick or a fraud, that they made a fundamental mistake as to the nature of the document and that they were not careless in signing it. The mistake made by the signee must concern the actual nature of the contract and not just its legal effect.

Mutual and unilateral mistakes

These mistakes negate consent, that is they prevent the formation of an agreement. The courts adopt an objective test in deciding whether agreement has been reached. It is not enough for one of the parties to allege that he was mistaken. Mistake can negate consent in the following cases.

Mutual mistakes concerning the identity of the subject matter

In these cases the parties are at cross-purposes, but there must have been some ambiguity in the situation before the courts will declare the contracts void. One such case that illustrates this is Raffles v Wichelhaus (1864) where a consignment of cotton was bought to arrive on the ship *Peerless* from Bombay. Two ships, both called Peerless, were due to leave Bombay at around the same time.

It was held that there was no agreement as the buyer was thinking of one ship and the seller was referring to the other ship.

Unilateral mistake concerning the terms of the contract

Here, one party has taken advantage of the other party's error. In Hartog v Colin and Shields (1939) the sellers mistakenly offered to sell goods at a given price per pound when they intended to offer them per piece. All the preliminary negotiations had been on a per piece basis. The buyers must have realised that the sellers had made a mistake. It was held that the contract was void.

Unilateral mistakes as to the identities of other parties to the contract

Where the identity of the other party is of fundamental importance, and there has been a genuine mistake, the contract will be void. In Cundy v Lindsey (1878) a Mr Blenkarn ordered goods from Lindsey signing the letter to give the impression that the order came from Blenkiron and Co, a firm known as Lindsey and Co. It was held that the contract was void. Linsey and Co had only intended to do business with Blenkiron and Co. there was therefore a mistake concerning the identity of the other party to the contract.

A mistake as to attributes or credit-worthiness will not render a contract void. In Kings Norton Metal Co v Edridge Merrett and Co Ltd (1872) a Mr Wallis ordered goods on impressive stationary which indicated that the order had come from Hallam and Co, an old established firm with branches all over the country. It was held that the contract was not void. The sellers intended to do business with the writer of the letter; they were merely mistaken as to his attributes, that is, the size and credit worthiness of his business.

Another case illustrating this is Boulton v Jones (1857) where the defendant sent an order for some goods to a Mr Brocklehurst unaware that he had sold his business to his foreman, the plaintiff. The plaintiff supplied the goods but the defendant refused to pay for them as he had only intended to do business with Brocklehurst, against whom he had a set off. It was held that there was a mistake concerning the identity of the other party and the contract was therefore void.

Mistake in equity

The narrow approach taken by the common law towards remedies for mistake (that is that it renders the contract void) is supplemented by the more flexible approach of equity. The following remedies may be available in equity: rescission (discussed above); rectification and refusal of specific performance.

Rectification

Where some aspect of a written document is alleged not to reflect accurately the will of the parties, the remedy of rectification may in certain instances allow the written document to be altered so that it coincides with the true agreement of the parties. In order for this remedy to be applied, three conditions must be satisfied: the parties must have agreed about the point in question; the agreement on that aspect of the contract must have continued unchanged up to the time it was put into writing and the written document must fail to express the parties agreement on that point.

****

1.5

CONTRACTS AND ILLEGALITY

Although a contract, on the face of it may contain all the elements of a valid agreement, such as offer and consideration, that contract may still be legally unenforceable.

Contracts may be illegal at the time of their formation or because of the way they have been performed. A contract may be illegal when entered into because the contract cannot be performed in accordance with its terms without committing an illegal act. For example, a contract may involve a breach of the criminal law, or it may be a statutory requirement for the parties to the contract to have a license that they in fact do not have. A case that illustrates this is Levy v Yates (1838). In this case, there existed a statutory rule that a royal license was required to perform a play within 20 miles of London. In that case the contract was between a theatre owner and an impresario for the performance of a theatrical production where no royal license had been obtained. The contract was thus illegal at the time of its formation.

Illegal mode of performance

In some cases a contract may be perfectly legal when it was made, but may be carried out in an illegal manner. A case that illustrates this is Anderson Ltd v Daniel (1924). In this case, a statute provided that a seller of artificial fertilizer had to supply buyers with an invoice detailing certain chemicals used in its manufacture. The sellers failed to provide the invoice needed. Although not against the law to sell fertilizer it was against statutory rules not to supply an invoice. As a result the sellers were unable to claim the price when the defendants refused to pay. A contract is obviously illegal if it involves a contravention of the law. However, a contract is also regarded as being illegal where it involves conduct that the law disapproves of as contrary to the interests of the public, even though the conduct is not actually unlawful. In both cases the transaction is treated as an illegal contract and the courts will not enforce it.

Contracts violating legal rules-Breach of common law

There are a number of factors that may make a contract illegal at common law, the most important where there is a contract to commit a crime or tort (negligent act). These are obvious breaches of the law. However, another very important area is contracts in restraint of trade. The issue of restraint of trade commonly arises and concerns those contracts that limit an individuals right to use their skills for payment, or to trade freely. These contracts fall into four groups:

- Contracts for the sale of a business where the vendor promises not to compete with the purchaser
- Contracts between businesses by which prices or output are regulated
- Contracts in which an employee agrees that on leaving employment they will not set up in business or be employed in such as way as to compete with their employer or ex employer. This is most common in business where personal skills and reputation attract custom, such as advertising and the ex-employee may take with them valuable customers
- Contracts where a person agrees to restrict their mode of trade by, for example, only accepting orders from one particular company. This is sometimes called a 'solus' agreement and is frequently used for petrol stations, in return for the land or lease the trader promises to use the product of the seller (Esso Petroleum v Harper's Garage (Stourport) 1968).

Any of the above can be held to create a restraint of trade, a general restraint if the contract completely prohibits trading, or a partial restraint if it limits trading to a certain time or area.

Breach of legislation

Some types of contract are expressly declared void by statute. The two most

46

important examples of contracts that are expressly declared void by statute are contracts in constraint of trade and wagering contracts.

Contracts in restraint of trade

As stated above, these are arrangements by which one party agrees to limit his or her legal right to carry out a trade, business or profession. A contract that does this is always viewed as *prima facie* void for two reasons:

- To prevent people signing away their livelihoods at the request of a party with stronger bargaining power
- To avoid depriving the public of the person's expertise.

These contracts are of several possible types as mentioned above-employee restraints, vendor restraints-preventing the seller of a business from unfairly competing with the purchaser and agreements of mutual regulation between businesses.

However, these agreements might be upheld as reasonable:

- as between the patties-so the restraint must be no wider than to protect a legitimate interest
- in the public interest-so the restraint must not unduly limit public choice.

The reasonableness of the restraint is also measured against factors such as duration and geographical extent.

Employee restraints

An employer can legitimately protect trade secrets and client connection, but not merely prevent the employee from exercising his or her trade or skill.

Reasonableness is measured against certain criteria:

- A restraint in a highly specialised business is more likely to be reasonable. In the case of Forster and Sons Ltd. v. Suggett (1918) 35 TLR 87 the works manager of the plaintiff who were chiefly engaged in making glass and glass bottles was instructed, in certain confidential me those concerning inter alia the correct mixture of gas and air in the furnaces. He agreed that during the five years following the determination of his employment he would not carry on in the United Kingdom or be interested in glass bottle manufacture or in any other business connected with glass making as conducted by the plaintiffs. The restraint for protection of trade secrets was held to be reasonable.

- Restraint of an employee in a key position is more likely to be reasonable.

An employer is not entitled to protect itself against the use of the skill and knowledge which the employee acquired during his or her employment. Those belong to the employee, who must be free to exploit them in the market place. Neither can an employer seek protection from competition per se since it is against the public interest that employees should be deprived of the opportunity to earn their living or to use their personal skills to the ultimate benefit of the community as a whole:

Herbert Morris Limited v Saxelby
[1916] AC 688.

Instead the employer must demonstrate that the covenant protects a legitimate business interest. In the Herbert Morris case, Lord Parker defined this as "some proprietary right, whether in the nature of a trade connection or in the nature of trade secrets, for the protection of which such a restraint is reasonably necessary".

The concept was further developed by Lord Wilberforce in Stenhouse Australia Limited v Phillips [1974] 1 All ER 117, who said:

"The employer's claim for protection must be based on the identification of some advantage or asset inherent in the business which can properly be regarded as, in a general sense, his property, and which it would be unjust to allow the employee to appropriate for his own purposes, even though he (the employee) may have contributed to its creation".

In other words, the employer is entitled to prevent the employee taking unfair advantage of confidential information and business connections to which he had access in the course of his/her employment

An employee may be significant to the business without even being a member of staff as demonstrated in Leeds rugby Ltd v Harris (2005).

The duration of the extent must not be too long (Home Counties Dairies v Skilton (1970) and the geographical extent too wide (Fitch v Dewes (1921). Similarly, the range of activities that the restraint covers must be no wider than is necessary to protect legitimate interests (J A Mont (UK) Ltd v Mills (1993).

Soliciting of clients can be prevented by such clauses, if not too wide (M&S Drapers v Reynolds (1957). Also, including clients not within the original scope of the restraint is not unreasonable (Hanover Insurance Brokers Ltd and Christchurch Insurance Brokers Ltd v Shapiro (1994). Attempting a restraint by other means is also void, including making contractual benefits subject to a restraint (Bull v Pitney Bowes Ltd (1966) and restraints in rules of associations (Eastham v Newcastle United FC Ltd (1963).

Vendor restraints

These are void for public policy to prevent an individual from negotiating away his or her livelihood and also because the public may lose a valuable service. Restraints are more likely to be upheld as reasonable since businesses deal on more equal bargaining strength, even is restraint is very wide (Nordenfelt v Maxim Nordenfelt Co (1894).

The restraint must still protect a legitimate interest to be valid (British Concrete Ltd v Schelff (1921).

Agreements between merchants, manufacturers or other trades

If the object is regulation of trade then they are void unless both sides benefit (English Hop Growers v Dering (1928). So they are void when the parties have unequal bargaining strength (Schroder Publishing Co Ltd v Macaulay (1974)-unless public policy dictates otherwise Panayiotou v Sony Music International (UK) Ltd (1994).

Wagering contracts

Wagering agreements are bets, and are rendered void by The Gaming Act 1845. Section 18 of the Act provides: "All contracts or agreements, whether by parole or in writing, by way of gaming or wagering, shall be null and void, and no suit shall be brought or maintained in a court of law or equity for recovering any sum of money or valuable thing alleged to be won upon any wager…"

The Act does not make wagering agreements illegal it simply provides that neither party to such an agreement can legally enforce it. For the provisions of the legislation to apply, a wagering contract must be one in which there are two parties and the terms of the agreement are such that one party wins and the other loses. This means that football pools, for example, are not covered as its promoters take a percentage of the stake money and so gain by the transaction regardless of whether players win as well. The Act also covers gaming, which is defined by the Betting, Gaming and lotteries act 1963 as 'the playing of a game of chance for winnings in money or money's worth'. Games of chance include games that depend partly on skill and partly on chance. Athletic games and sports are excluded.

Competition law

Common law lays down certain controls on contracts in constraint of trade. These controls give only limited protection and actual legislation provides more adequate protection. One of the main goals of the European Union, through Article 85, is to promote free trade between member states and clearly restrictive trade can affect this policy. Where a restrictive trade agreement could affect trade between member states it will only be valid if allowed under both EU and English law. In terms of contracts in English law, the relevant legislation is now contained in the Competition Act 1998. This Act prohibits a number of anti-competitive practices. The 1998 Act applies to agreements between undertakings, decisions by associations of undertakings or concerted practices that (a) may affect trade and (b) have as their object or effect the prevention, restriction or distortion of trade. For the Act to prohibit an agreement the effect of the agreement must be significant and not minor.

Contracts against public policy

There exist a wide-range of contracts that are considered to be illegal because they are against public policy. As we discussed, public policy really means the interest of society at large and the contract must contravene it. Contracts promoting sexual immorality for example are seen as contravening public policy.

One case that illustrates this is Armhouse Lee Ltd v Chappell (1996) concerning a contract under which the defendants paid the plaintiffs to place adverts for telephone sex lines in magazines. When regulation concerning such publicity was tightened the defendants terminated the contract, as they no longer wished to advertise their services in this way. The plaintiffs brought an action for the money due under the contract and the defendants argued that the contract was illegal and unenforceable as it promoted sexual immorality. This defense was rejected by the Court of Appeal. The court held that though the adverts were distasteful the sex lines were generally accepted by society and were regulated by the telephone industry. There was no evidence, in the eyes of the Court of Appeal that any 'generally accepted moral code' condemned these telephone sex lines. It considered that contracts should only be found illegal under this heading if an element of public harm clearly existed.

Contracts prejudicial to public safety

The main types of contracts found illegal on these grounds are contracts with those living in an enemy country, contracts to perform acts which are illegal in a friendly foreign country and contracts which are damaging to foreign relations.

The effect of an illegal contract

The effect of an illegal contract will depend on whether it is illegal due to a statute or due to the common law. Where the contract is illegal due to a statute, in some cases the statute provides for the consequences of any illegality. Under common law an illegal contract is void and courts will not order it to be performed.

The precise effects of an illegal contract depend on whether the contract is illegal at the time of formation or is illegal due to the way in which it was performed. Contracts illegal at the time of formation are treated as if they were never made, so the illegal contract is unenforceable by either party. Contracts illegal as performed are slightly different as to their effect. It will be possible to enforce the illegal contract if the illegal act was merely incidental to the performance of the contract. For example, a contract for the delivery of goods may not be tainted by illegality when the lorry driver is caught speeding or under the influence of drink. Where the contract is merely illegal because of the way it was performed, it is possible for either both or only one of the parties to intend illegal performance. If both parties are aware that a contracts performance is illegal, the consequences for this type of contract are the same as for a contract that was illegal at the time of its formation. When one party did not know of the illegal performance of the contract by the other party, the innocent party can enforce it.

In some cases, it is possible to divide the illegal part of a contract from the rest and enforce the provisions which are not affected by the illegality-this is called severance. The illegal parts of the contract can be severed if they are relatively unimportant to the contract and if the severance leaves the nature of the contract unaltered.

****

1.6

DURESS AND UNDUE INFLUENCE

As we have seen, contracts are only binding if parties voluntarily consent to them. If one party is forced to sign under duress, the contract is invalid. As is usual, the law has developed two doctrines to deal with duress: the common law of duress and the equitable one of undue influence.

Duress

Although traditionally, common law has dealt with duress in terms of physical or psychological duress exerted when signing a contract, the doctrine has now been extended to economic duress. This, as the term implies, is where one party is forced into the contract due to economic pressure. Economic duress first arose in North Ocean Shipping Co v Hyundai Construction Co (The Atlantic Baron) (1979) that concerned a contract for the building of a ship. As is commonly the case where duress is raised, the dispute concerned not the formation of the contract, but a supposed modification of its terms. Such a modification can only be binding if both parties consent to it. If one party's consent is achieved by duress the contract is void. Although the price of the ship had been fixed at the outset` while it was being built the sellers decided to raise the price by ten per cent, due to a drop in the exchange rate of the dollar. The buyers were not happy about this but were unwilling to risk delaying completion of the ship as they were already negotiating for it to be chartered by a major oil company. They therefore agreed to pay the increased price.

Eight months after the ship was delivered the buyers tried to sue the sellers claiming back the ten per cent because they said that it had been extracted from them under duress. The judge agreed that economic power constituted duress, the question being whether there had been 'compulsion of will'. This compulsion could stem from economic pressure as well as physical force. In this particular case the buyers were not allowed to recover the extra ten per cent. This was not because duress did not play a part as it did, but that they waited so long after delivery to sue, implying acceptance.

Economic duress will be present where there is compulsion of will to the extent that the party under threat has no practical alternative but to comply, and the pressure used is regarded by the law as illegitimate.

Compulsion or coercion of the will

In Pau v Lau Yiu Long (1980) Lord Scarman listed the following indications of compulsion or coercion of the will:

- Did the party coerced have an alternative course open to him
- Did the party coerced protest
- Did the party coerced have independent advice?
- Did the party coerced take steps to avoid the contract?

Undue influence

Undue influence is an equitable doctrine, which applies where one party uses their influence over another to persuade them to make a contract. Where a court finds that a contract was made as a result of undue influence, it may set it aside, or modify its terms. In Bank of Credit and Commerce International SA v Aboody (1990) The court distinguished between two classes of undue influence: actual and presumed.

Class 1. Actual undue influence arises where the claimant can prove that they entered into the transaction as a result of undue influence from the other party. An example is where a person promises to either pay money or give goods in exchange for a promise not to report them for a criminal offence. The party claiming duress must prove that they were influenced (Williams v Bayley (1886)).

Class 2. Presumed undue influence will arise where there is a pre-existing relationship between the parties to a contract, as a result of which one places trust in another, and the contract between them is obviously disadvantageous to the one placing trust in another. Such a relationship of trust is called a fiduciary relationship and it may arise in two ways. It may fall into a category in which a relationship of trust is presumed to exist, such as parent and children (Lancashire Loans Co v Black (1933)) patient-doctor, solicitor and client, trustees and beneficiaries (Benningfield v Baxter (1886)) and spiritual leaders and followers (Allcard v Skinner (1887)). Where a relationship does not fall into obvious categories then a relationship of trust may well be established through, for example, effluxion of time or inherent trust such as an ongoing successful business relationship. Where there has been a long relationship of trust and confidence between the parties, and the transaction is not readily explicable by the nature of the relationship, for example, between husband and wife or where one party had been accustomed to rely for advice and guidance on the other, the presumption in these cases of trust and confidence is irrebuttable. The presumption of undue influence where the transaction 'calls for explanation' is rebuttable. The stronger party can rebut the presumption of undue influence by showing that:

- full disclosure of all material facts was made
- the consideration was adequate
- the weaker party was in receipt of independent legal advice

One example of a fiduciary relationship is in the case of Lloyds Bank v Bundy (1974). The plaintiff and his son both used the same bank. The son ran into business difficulties and the father was asked to guarantee the overdraft. He did this, putting up his farm as a guarantee and the bank tried to repossess the farm. The farmer claimed that the contract had been obtained by undue influence, on the basis that he had banked with Lloyds for a long time, and in that time had placed considerable trust in their advice, yet they had made no effort to warn him that it was not in their interest to give the guarantee. The Court of Appeal agreed that the presumption of undue influence had been raised. There was a relationship based on trust over time and the bank lost the case. The transaction must be extremely disadvantageous (manifestly so) to give rise to a presumption of undue influence. This will be the case where it would have been 'obvious to any independent and reasonable persons who considered the transaction at that time with knowledge of all the relevant facts'. (Bank of Credit and Commerce International SA v Aboody (1989)).

Inequality of bargaining power

In Lloyds Bank v Bundy, as described above, Lord Denning suggested that economic duress was simply an example of a general principle of inequality of bargaining power. He argued that this principle allows English law to give relief to anyone who, without taking independent advice, makes a contract on unfair terms, or sells property for much less than it is worth because their own bargaining power is seriously compromised by ignorance, infirmity or need. Clearly, this is a key principle when negotiating and entering into contracts, more pertinent than simple undue influence as there is no suggestion that the other party had behaved improperly.

Illegitimate pressure

There must be some element of illegitimacy in the pressure exerted, for example, a threatened breach of contract. The illegitimacy will normally arise from the fact that what was threatened is unlawful. Economic duress is often pleaded together with lack of consideration in cases where a breach of consent is threatened by the promisor, unless he receives additional payment.

One case that illustrates this is Atlas Express v Kafco (1989) where Kafco, a small company which imported and distributed basketware, had a contract to supply Woolworths. They contracted with Atlas for the delivery of the basketware to Woolworths. The contract commenced, then Atlas discovered that they had underpriced the contract, and told Kafco that unless they paid a minimum sum for each consignment, they would cease to deliver. Kafco were heavily dependent on the Woolworth contract, and knew that a failure to deliver would lead both to the loss of the contract and an action for damages. At that time of year, they could not find an alternative carrier and agreed, under protest, to make the extra payments. Atlas sued for kafco's non-payment. It was held that the agreement was invalid for economic duress, and also for lack of consideration..

Manifest disadvantage

In any claim of presumed undue influence, the agreement must be manifestly disadvantageous. In deciding whether an agreement is manifestly disadvantageous the courts will look at whether the disadvantages of the transaction outweigh the advantages.

Effect of undue influence on a third party

A bank may be deemed to have constructive knowledge of an impropriety if it has been placed 'on inquiry' that one of the parties has unduly influenced the other into entering into the contract. The leading case on undue influence is Royal bank of Scotland v Etridge (2001). This appeal concerned eight cases of undue influence. In seven cases, the wife had permitted the family home, of which she had part ownership to be used as surety against her husband's personal or business debts. In all cases, the husband had defaulted and the bank had sought possession of the family home. The wife claimed that the bank had been placed on enquiry that the agreement had been elicited as a result of the husband's undue influence. It was held that three appeals were dismissed and five allowed. Moreover, the House of Lords provided important guidance for banks on how to avoid constructive knowledge of undue influence. The HOL also held that in that situation the third party could discharge his duty by making clear to the party concerned the full nature of the risk he or she is taking on.

****

1.7

DISCHARGE OF A CONTRACT

A contract is said to be discharged when the rights and obligations in it come to an end. There are four ways in which a contract can come to an end: performance under the contract, i.e., natural end, end by mutual agreement, breach of contract and frustration. We should look at these areas in turn.

Performance under contract

This is the most obvious way of parties discharging their obligations and bringing the contract to a satisfactory end. In many cases, it is uncomplicated but there are some cases where one party may claim to have discharged their obligations and the other party disagrees. The law then has to look at the question of what constitutes performance.

The obvious and general rule is that performance must exactly match the requirements laid down in the contract. This is known as entire performance. If the first party fails to perform then the other party need pay nothing at all, even if the shortfall actually causes no hardship. This is the simple rule and obviously contracts can be more complicated, with claim and counter claim. The case of Cutter v Powell (1795) demonstrates the difficulty. A sailor had contracted to serve on a ship traveling from Jamaica to Liverpool. He was to be paid 30 Guineas for the voyage, payable when the ship arrived in Liverpool. However, he died during the journey. His widow sued for wages up until he died, but her claim was unsuccessful, as the court held that the contract required entire performance.

Similarly, in Bolton v Mahadeva (1972) a central heating system gave out less heat than it should, and there were fumes in one room. It was held that the contractor could not claim payment; although the boiler and pipes had been installed, they did not fulfill the primary purpose of heating the house.

The rule can also allow parties to escape from what has become an

59

unprofitable contract to do so by taking advantage of the most minor departures from its terms. In Re Moore and Co Ltd and Landaur and Co (1921) the contract concerned the sale of canned fruit that were to be packed into cases of 30 tins. On delivery it was discovered that although the correct number of tins had been sent, almost half the cases contained only 24 tins in each. This made no difference to the market value of the goods, but the buyers pointed out that the sale was covered by the Sale of Goods Act, which stated that goods sold by description must correspond with that description. The delivery did not, and the buyers were within their rights to reject the whole consignment.

Mitigation of the entire performance rule
Substantial performance
This doctrine allows a party who has performed with only minor defects to claim the price of the work done, less any money the other party will have to spend to put the defects right.

Severable contracts
A contract is said to be severable where payment becomes due at various stages of performance, rather than in one lump sum when performance is complete. Most contracts of employment are examples of this. Also, major building contracts also operate in this way, allowing for stage payments. In a severable contract the money due at the end of each stage may be claimed and the person carrying out the work under the contract can refuse to continue if the payments are not made.

Prevention of performance by one party
Where one party performs one part of the agreed obligation, and is then prevented from completing the rest of the contract because of a fault of the other party, a quantum meruit can be claimed from the other party. Quantum meruit is an assessment of the amount performed to date and a reasonable price arrived at.

Breach of terms concerning time

The judgment here will be that of an assessment of whether 'time is of the essence' and the effect that completing the contract out of time has on the other party.

Frustration of contract

The basic principle underlying frustration of contract is that, after a contract is made, something happens, through no fault of the parties own, to make fulfillment of the contract impossible. Although there are many situations that can make it impossible to fulfill a contract only certain cases can be seen as genuine frustration.

The modern doctrine of frustration arose from Taylor v Caldwell (1863). The parties in the case had entered into an agreement concerning the use of Surrey Gardens and music hall for a series of concerts and day and night fetes. Six days before the planned date for the first concert, the building was burnt down, making it impossible for the concerts to go ahead. The party planning to put on the concerts was sued for breach of contract but the action failed, as fulfillment of the contract was impossible.

The concept and practice of frustration of contract can be placed in three categories: events that make performance or further performance impossible; events that make performance illegal; and those that make it pointless.

Impossible to fulfill contract

A contract may become impossible to perform because of destruction or unavailability of something essential for the contract to be performed.

Death of either party to the contract

Unavailability of party. Contracts which require personal performance will be frustrated if one party, for example, is ill or is imprisoned, providing that the non-availability of the party substantially effects performance

Method of performance impossible

Where a contract lays down a particular method of performance and this becomes impossible, the contract may be frustrated. A contract is unlikely to be frustrated simply because performance has become more expensive or more onerous than expected. The leading modern case on frustration is Davis Contractors Co Ltd v Fareham UDC (1956). Davis, a construction company contracted to build 78 houses for a local authority. The job was to take eight months, at a price of £94,000. In fact, labor shortages delayed the work, which ended up taking 22 months and cost the builders £22,000 more than they had planned for. The defendant was willing to pay the contract price in spite of the delay, but Davis sought to have the contract discharged on the grounds of frustration arguing that labor shortages made performance fundamentally different from that envisaged in the contract (it intended to seek payment on a quantum meruit basis to cover costs).

However, the House of Lords decided that the events that caused the delays were within the range of changes that could reasonably be expected to happen during the performance of a contract for building houses and the change of circumstances did not make performance radically different from what was expected. Therefore, the contract was not frustrated. Lord Radcliffe explained:

'it is not hardship or inconvenience or material loss which itself calls the principle of frustration into play. There must be as well such a change in the significance of the obligation that the thing undertaken would, if performed, be different from that contracted for'.

Illegality

If, after a contract is formed, a change in the law makes its performance illegal, the contract will be frustrated.

Performance made pointless

A contract can be frustrated where a supervening event makes performance of a contract completely pointless, though still technically possible. A contract can be rendered pointless if there has been such a drastic change of circumstances as to dramatically alter the nature of the contract.

Time of frustrating event

In order to frustrate a contract, the event in question must occur after the contract is made.

Limits to the doctrine of frustration

The doctrine of frustration will not be applied on the grounds of inconvenience, increase in expense or loss of profit. The case above that highlights this is Davis Contractors Limited v Fareham UDC (1956).

It will also not apply where there is express provision in the contract covering the intervening event or where the frustration is self-induced.

A contract will not be frustrated if the event making performance impossible was the voluntary action of one party. If the party concerned had a choice open to him, and chose to act as to make performance impossible, then frustration will be self induced and the court will refuse to treat the contract as discharged. One such case that highlights this is The Superservant Two (1990). In this case one of the two barges owned by the defendants and used to transport oil rigs was sunk. They were therefore unable to fulfill their contract to transport an oil rig belonging to the plaintiff as their other barge (superservant one) was already allocated to other contracts. It was held that the contract was not frustrated. The defendants had another barge available, but chose not to allocate it to the contract with the plaintiffs.

Where the event was foreseeable

If, by reason of special knowledge, the event was foreseeable by one party, then he cannot claim frustration. This was highlighted in Amalgamated Investment and Property Co v John Walker and Sons Ltd (1976) where the possibility that a building could be listed was foreseen by the plaintiff who had enquired about the matter beforehand. A failure to obtain planning permission was also foreseeable and was a normal risk for property developers. The contract was therefore not frustrated.

Breach of contract

A contract is breached when one party performs defectively, or differently from the agreement or not at all (actual breach) or indicates in advance that they will not be performing as agreed (anticipatory breach). Where an anticipatory breach occurs, the other party can sue for breach straight away, it is not necessary to wait until performance falls due.

One case illustrating this is Frost v Knight (1872) where the defendant had promised to marry the plaintiff once his father had died. He later broke off the engagement before his father died, and when his ex fiancé sued him for breach of promise, he argued that she had no claim as the time for performance had not yet arrived. This argument was rejected and the plaintiff's case succeeded. Any effect of a breach of contract will entitle the innocent party to sue for damages but not every breach will entitle the wronged party to discharge the contract. If the contract is not discharged it will still need to be performed.

There are three main circumstances where the innocent party may wish to seek to discharge the contract:

Repudiation – this is where one party makes it clear that they no longer wish to be bound by the contract, either during its performance or before performance is due

Breach of a condition – Breach of a condition allows the innocent party to terminate the contract.

Serious breach of an innominate term- where the relevant term is classified as innominate, it will be the one that can be breached in both serious and trivial ways, and whether the innocent party is entitled to terminate or not will depend on how serious the results of the breach are. If the results are so serious as to undermine the foundations of the contract, the innocent party will have the right to terminate.

Even when one of these three types of breach occurs, the contract is not automatically discharged. The innocent party can usually choose whether or not to terminate. If the innocent party chooses to terminate this must be clearly communicated to the other party.

64

Agreement

In some cases, the parties to a contract will simply agree to terminate the contract, so that one or both parties are released from their obligations. A distinction is usually made between bilateral discharge where both parties will benefit from the ending by agreement and a unilateral discharge where one party benefits. In general an agreed discharge will be binding if it contains the same elements that make a contract binding when it is formed. Those that present the most problems are formality and consideration.

Consideration

Consideration is not usually a problem where both parties agree to alter their obligations since each is giving something in return for the change. Problems are most likely to occur when one parties obligations change. If the other party agrees to the change, their agreement will only be binding if put into the form of a deed, or supported by consideration. Where consideration is provided in return for one party's agreement to change this is called 'accord'. The provision of consideration is called 'satisfaction'. The arrangement is often termed accord and satisfaction.

Formalities

This issue arises in connection with certain types of contract (mainly concerning the sale of land) that must be evidenced in writing to be binding under the Law of Property Act (1925).

Remedies for breach of contract

There are a number of remedies available to the innocent party in the event of a breached contract. There are two main remedies, those under common law and equitable remedies. There is a third category that involves remedies arising from the party's own agreement.

1.8

REMEDIES FOR BREACH OF CONTRACT

The usual Remedy for breach of contracts is the award of damages to the innocent party. It aims to compensate for losses that result from not receiving performance that was due under the contract. In general the damages will cover both physical harm to the claimant and their property and also for any economic loss. There are very limited circumstances in which injury to feelings can be compensated for.

Damages can fall into the categories of unliquidated damages, which are damages assessed by the courts, the purpose of which is to compensate the victim for the loss he has suffered as a result of the breach and liquidated damages where the damages are set by the parties themselves.

When considering damages the general rule is that any damages are awarded innocent parties will place them in a position they would have been if the contract had been performed. There are, however, three limitations: causation, remoteness and mitigation.

Causation

A person will be liable only for losses caused by their own breach of contract. Acts intervening between the breach of contract and the loss incurred may break the chain of causation. One case illustrating this is County Ltd v Girozentrale Securities (1996) where the plaintiff's bank agreed to underwrite the issue of 26 million shares in a publicly quoted company. The defendants were stockbrokers who were engaged by the plaintiffs to approach potential investors in the shares. The brokers breached the terms of their contract and, in due course, the plaintiffs found themselves with 4.5 million shares on their hands which, the price of shares having fallen, represented a loss of nearly £7.5m. They sued the stockbrokers and the main issue in the case was whether the plaintiff's loss was caused by the defendant's breach of contract. In effect the plaintiffs would not have suffered their loss if there had not been a concurrence of a number of events of which the defendant's breach of contract was one. The Court of Appeal held that the broker's breach of contract remained the effective cause of the plaintiff's loss, the breach did not need to be the only cause. The defendants were liable for damages.

Remoteness

There are some losses that clearly result from the defendant's breach of contract, but are considered too remote from the breach for compensation to arise.

The rules concerning remoteness were originally laid down in Hadley v Baxendale (1854). The case concerned a contract for delivery of an important piece of mill equipment, which had been sent away for repair. The equipment, an iron shaft, was not delivered until some days after the agreed date, which meant that the mill, which could not work without it, stood idle for the period whilst awaiting the part. The mill owners attempted to sue for this loss. The courts held that the defendant could not be liable for the loss in this case.

Mitigation

Claimants cannot simply sit back, do nothing, and let losses pile up and expect compensation for the whole loss if there was something that could have been done to mitigate the loss. It is up to defendants in this case to prove that the loss could have been mitigated. Claimants need only do what is reasonable to mitigate the loss.

Calculating any loss

Once it has been established that there is a loss and the defendant is liable the court must quantify the damages. In 1936, two American academics, Fuller and Perdue came up with two main ways of calculating compensation:

Loss of expectation (also called loss of bargain). This is the usual way in which contract damages are calculated and it aims to put claimants in the position that they would have been if the contract had not been performed.

Reliance loss. There are some cases of loss that are very difficult to quantify and in this case, the court may award damages calculated to compensate for any expenses or other loss incurred by the claimant when relying on the contract.

Action for an agreed sum

Where a contract specifies a price to be paid for performance, and the party due to pay fails to do so, the party who has performed can claim the price owing by means of an action for the agreed sum. Although the claim is for money this is not the same as a claim for damages. The claimant is not seeking compensation, but simply enforcement of the defendants promise to pay. However, where the claimant has suffered additional loss beyond not receiving the agreed price, damages can be claimed alongside the agreed sum. An action such as this can only be brought once the duty to pay has arisen

Restitution

Where money has been paid under a contract or purported contract and performance has not been received in return, or has not been adequate, the payer may want to claim the money back, rather than claiming damages (if, for example, no additional loss has resulted from the failure to perform). In general this will only be possible if there has been a total failure of consideration so that restitution will prevent undue enrichment. This means that the party paying the money has not received any of what was paid for.

Equitable remedies

Where common law remedies are inadequate to compensate the claimant, there is a range of equitable remedies. However, these are not available as of right, merely because the defendant is in breach. They are provided at the discretion of the court, taking into account the behavior of both parties and the overall circumstances.

Specific performance

The common law will not force a specific party in breach to perform (except where performance is paying money only), even though this might be a fairly obvious solution to many contract problems. However, the equitable remedy of specific performance does compel a party in breach to perform. In practice, specific performance rarely applies as the making of such an order is subject to certain restrictions. Specific performance is only granted if damages alone would be an inadequate remedy Specific performance is mainly applied to contracts to sell land since each piece of land is thought to be unique and impossible to replace. Where the damages are only nominal specific performance may be ordered to stop one party becoming unjustly enriched.

Because specific performance is a discretionary remedy the court will not apply it to cases where it could cause the claimant great hardship or unfairness. The courts will also allow the courts to refuse specific performance of a contract that has been obtained by unfair means. Some types of contract are unsuitable for specific performance, the two main types being contracts involving personal services (such as employment contracts) and contracts that involve continuous duties.

Injunctions

Another remedy is that of the injunction. An injunction orders the defendant not to do a specific thing. Where the contract has already been breached the courts can make a mandatory injunction that will order the defendant to restore the situation to what it was before the breach.

Types of injunction

There are three main types of injunction, prohibitory injunction, which is an order commanding the defendant not to do something: mandatory injunction which orders the defendant to undo something he had agreed not to; interim injunction which is designed to regulate the position of the parties pending trial.

Injunctions are also discretionary remedies and are subject to the similar constraints of orders of specific performance. However, an injunction will be granted to enforce a negative stipulation in a contract of employment, as long as this is not an indirect way of enforcing the contract.

Two cases highlighting this are:

Warner Brother Pictures Inc v Nelson (1937) where the actress Bette Davis was contracted to WB exclusively for a one year period, with an option to extend the period. During the period of contract she agreed to act for a competitor of WB. The court granted an injunction which prevented her from working for the competitor.

Page One Records v Britton (1968) where the 1960's pop group, The Troggs, were prevented indefinitely by their contract form appointing another person to work as their manager. The group were dissatisfied with their manager and appointed another. The courts refused to grant an injunction as it would prevent the group from working as musicians or would tie them to a personal contract against their wishes.

Remedies agreed by the parties

Many contracts specify the kind of breach that will justify termination and the damages to be paid. There are two types of contractual clauses concerning damages: liquidated damages and penalty clauses.

Liquidated damages is the term used where a contract specifies the amount of damages to be paid in the event of a breach, and this amount represents a genuine attempt to work out what the loss in the event if such a breach would be.

Penalty damages work in a different way. Some contracts, especially construction contracts, specify very high damages in the event of breach and they act as a deterrent, compelling the other party to perform. Where a court finds the damages laid down in contract act in this way, the relevant clause will be invalid and the party putting forward the clause must pursue damages in the usual way.

One case which illustrates this, and which provided for guidelines was that of Dunlop Pneumatic Tyre Co Ltd v New Garage and Motor Co Ltd (1915). The plaintiffs supplied tyres to the defendants under a contract providing that the defendants would not resell them at less than the list price. If they breached this provision they would be liable to pay £5 for every tyre sold at less than the list price. The House of Lords held that the provision was not penal and was in the nature of liquidated damages. Undercutting the list price would have been damaging to the plaintiff's business.

Lord Dunedin described the factors to be taken into account when deciding whether damages were penal or not, damages would be considered penal if the sum laid down was extravagantly greater than any loss that might conceivably result from the breach.

****

Ch.2

BUSINESS LAW-NEGLIGENCE AND DUTY OF CARE-GENERAL

In everyday parlance, negligence means a failure to pay attention to what ought to be done or to take the required level of care. Whereas its everyday usage implies a state of mind, the tort of negligence is concerned with the link between the defendant's behaviour and the risk that should have been foreseen.

Key definition of negligence

Negligence, as a tort, is generally defined as a breach of a duty of care. This duty of care is owed by one person to another. When damage is caused to a person, who then becomes a claimant, the type of damage has to be specified and also defined as actionable.

The loss or damage can arise in a number of ways, arising through misfeasance or nonfeasance and can consist of personal injury, damage to property or can be pure economic loss. It can also consist of psychiatric damage.

The duty of care-establishment of a duty

Certain relationships between people, recognised by the law and developed by the law, give rise to a legal duty of care. The following are examples:

-
- Employer-employee
- Manufacturer to consumer
- Doctor-patient
- Solicitor-client

Essentially, carelessness by one party which affects another gives rise, or can give rise, to legal action by the injured party. It is up to the claimant to prove that damage has been caused and that the case falls into a specific situation that gives rise to a duty of care.

The neighbour principle
Donoghue v Stevenson 1932

Outside of the categories of established duty, a duty of care will be determined on the basis of individual circumstances.

One of the most prominent cases relating to Tort and negligence is that of *Donoghue v Stevenson* (HL 1932) In this case, Mrs Donoghue and friend visited a café and Mrs Donoghue's friend bought her a bottle of ginger beer. The bottle was made of opaque glass. When filling Mrs Donoghue's glass the remains of a decomposed a snail floated out of the bottle. Mrs Donoghue developed gastroenteritis as a result.

Mrs Donoghue brought an action against the manufacturer's of the ginger beer. Lord Atkin formulated a general principle in this case, the **neighbour principle**, for determining whether a duty of care should exist. He stated:

"You must take reasonable care to avoid acts or omissions which you can reasonably foresee would be likely to injure your neighbour. Who then, in law, is my neighbour? The answer seems to be persons who are so closely and directly affected by my act that I ought reasonably to have them in contemplation as being so affected when I am directing my mind to the acts or omissions which are called in question".

The manufacturers were found liable as they owed her a duty of care that the bottle did not contain foreign bodies which would damage her health.

This principle was a landmark and established negligence as an independent tort

Out of this judgement, which was further developed in the case of *Caparo Industries plc v Dickman* (1990), (which is further outlined below) also comes the concept of foresight, i.e. was the damage itself reasonably foreseeable. There must be a legal relationship of 'sufficient proximity' between the parties. There is also a requirement that it is 'just and reasonable' to impose a duty on the defendant.

Even where the courts are prepared to find that the circumstances are such as to be capable of giving rise to a duty of care, it is still likely that the claimant in a case could fail if he or she was an 'unforeseeable victim' of the defendants negligence.

One such case which amplifies this is *Bourhill v Young* (1943) where the plaintiff in the case heard, but did not actually see a crash caused by the motorcyclists (the defendants) negligence. The plaintiff later saw part of the aftermath of the accident and sued the defendant after suffering nervous shock, and lost the case, as harm to her of that type was not foreseeable.

Essentially, the legal proximity of claimant to defendant must be clearly established. In *Davis v Radcliffe* (1990), for example, Lord Goff stated that proximity referred to such a relation between the parties as rendered it just and reasonable that a duty should be imposed. Lack of proximity can, in some cases, be attributed to the failure of just and reasonable requirement in a case. A variety of factors are considered, such as the status of the parties and their relationship with one another, nature of injury or harm suffered and the particular way that the harm arises. One seminal case which further defined the boundaries of tort and negligence was that of *Hedley Byrne and Co v Heller and Partners Ltd* (1964). Lord Pearce observed:

"How wide the sphere of duty of care in negligence is to be laid depends primarily on the courts assessment of the demands of society for protection from the carelessness of others"

The case of Hedley Byrne concerned Economic loss through negligent information (see below).

Pure economic loss

Although financial loss incurred as a result of a negligent action against a person and property is normally recoverable, problems can arise with so called 'pure' economic loss, which is financial loss which has not been accompanied by any other damage. Cases of financial loss may arise as a result of either negligent information or advice, or of negligent conduct. In general, courts will assess these cases on a case-by-case basis, rather than rely purely on precedent.

Before the Hedley Byrne case, liability for negligent statements, or misstatements, which resulted in financial or other loss, existed in contract, in the tort of deceit or for breach of a fiduciary duty. In Hedley Byrne and Co v Heller and Partners Ltd the plaintiffs wanted to know if they could safely advance credit to their client, (A). The plaintiff's bankers sought references from the defendants (B) bankers, who gave favourable reports 'without responsibility'. The plaintiffs relied on the information and then suffered financial loss when A went into liquidation. In this case, it was held that no duty arose because of the disclaimer. However, importantly, in appropriate circumstances, a duty could arise.

It was accepted that reasonable foresight of the harm was not enough in itself, but that a 'special relationship' must exist where, to the defendants knowledge the plaintiff relied upon the defendants skill and judgement or his ability to make careful enquiry, and it was reasonable in the circumstances for the plaintiff to do so. The essence of Hedley and Byrne can therefore be equated with the concept of 'reasonable reliance'.

Another case highlighting the above is that of *Caparo Industries* where Lord Bridge said that in order for a duty to arise, it was necessary to show that the defendant knew that his statement would be communicated to the plaintiff, either as an individual or as a member of an identifiable class, specifically in connection with a transaction or transactions of a particular kind, and that the plaintiff would be very likely to rely on it in deciding whether or not to enter into a transaction.

Provided that the defendant is aware of the existence of the claimant either as an individual or as a member of an ascertainable class, there is no need that

76

the defendant knows the identity of the claimant. A vital ingredient of the duty is the defendant's knowledge (actual or constructive) of the purpose for which the information is required. In Caparo Industries it was held that, in preparing the audit of the accounts of a public company, the defendants owed no duty either to the plaintiffs either as potential investors or as existing shareholders. The purpose of the audit was to report to the shareholders to enable them to exercise their rights in the management of the company, not to provide information which might assist them in making investment decisions.

In contrast to the position of auditors, surveyors appointed to value a house for mortgage purposes may owe a duty to the purchaser even though the primary purpose of the valuation is to enable the lender to decide whether to advance a loan. This was illustrated in *Harris v Wyre Forest District Council* (1989). This has been justified on the basis that valuers are paid for their services at the mortgagor's expense and understand that a lot of purchasers rely on these reports.

Contributory negligence (disclaimers)

On the assumption that an appropriately worded disclaimer is brought to the claimant's notice, either before or at the time the statement is made, it can be argued that no duty arises because the claimant's reliance would not be reasonable.

However, according to the House of Lords in the case *Smith v Eric S Bush* (1989), the effect of ss.11 (3) and 13 (1) of the Unfair Contract Terms Act 1977 is to subject all exclusion notices which would at common law provide a reasonable defence to an action for negligence, to a test of reasonableness, as provided for in s2 (2) of the act (this only relates to business liability).

Contributory negligence, which is discussed further in the book, is in principle a defence and is available equally to a claim under the Misrepresentation Act 1967.

Third party reliance

There are certain situations in which a duty of care will be imposed on a person (A), who makes a statement to B, as a result that B acts upon it to another's detriment. It is well established, generally, that a solicitor owes no duty of care to third parties. However, this is not always the case. For example, in *White v Jones* (1995), a majority of the House of Lords held the defendant solicitors liable for failing to carry out their clients instructions regarding his will, with the result that the plaintiffs (the intended beneficiaries) lost their legacy.

The duty under White v Jones is not confined to cases relating to wills. In *Gorham v British Telecommunications plc* (CA 2000) an insurance company was held to owe a duty of care to the customer's dependant wife and family where he had intended to create a benefit for them on his death. It was also held in *Spring v Guardian Assurance plc* (HL 1994) that an employer supplying a reference about an employee to a prospective employer owes a duty to the employee to avoid making untrue statements negligently or expressing unfounded opinions, even if held honestly and believed to be true. In this case, it was the opinion of the majority of the Lords that economic loss in the form of failure to obtain employment was clearly foreseeable if a careless reference was given and there was clear proximity of relationship as between employer and employee, so that it was fair, just and reasonable that the law should impose a duty on the employer.

Negligent acts

Although there was originally no liability for pure economic loss caused by acts of negligence, the Hedley Byrne case made major inroads into this area and, although this case was originally confined to misstatements, a trend has developed towards the formulation of a wider principle, applying to both statements and acts.

Damage to third party property

In some cases, damages to property belonging to a third party may prevent the claimant from carrying on their business. In other cases, their contract with the third party may be adversely affected. In neither case can the claimant recover any damages because of a long established rule that no claim will lie in respect of foreseeable economic loss, unaccompanied by physical damage to the property in which the claimant has an interest, either proprietary or possessory.

Defective property

If a claimant has acquired property and discovers it is defective, and money has to be spent on repairing or replacing it, such economic loss can be recovered against a party who has a relevant contractual obligation with the defendant. The claimant cannot bring a claim within the ordinary principles of tort, i.e. those contained within Donoghue v Stevenson, because the claim is concerned with defective goods which can cause personal injury or damage to property rather than the defective product in question.

However, although this was traditionally the case, this fundamental principle was brought into question in the case of *Anns v Merton London Borough Council* (HL 1978). In this case, damages were held to be recoverable by a building owner against a local authority which had negligently inspected and approved defective foundations. In Anns, the decision was justified on the basis that the cause of action arose when the building became an imminent danger to the health and safety of the occupier, who could then recover the cost of averting the potential danger.

Another case which developed this principle was *Junior Books Ltd v Veitchi Co Ltd* (HL 1983). The defendants were held liable for the cost of replacing a defective good supplied by them, even though there was no danger to health and safety. This decision went a considerable way to recognising a general right of recovery for pure economic loss. However, cases following this one have made it very clear that no new principle has been established and each case is viewed on its own merit.

Following a number of cases, the whole issue was considered by the Court of Appeal in *Murphy v Brentwood District Council* (HL 1990). The Lords unanimously overruled the findings in Anns so far as it imposed a duty on local authorities, on the ground that where a defect in a building was discovered before any personal injury or damage to property other than the defective house itself had been done, the expense incurred by the building owner in rectifying the defect (including associated costs such as vacating the premises) was pure economic loss and therefore irrecoverable in tort.

There are problems with the decision in Murphy, however. It would seem clear enough that the builder may be liable in accordance with Donoghue v Stevenson principles where a latent defect causes personal injury or damage to another property. In addition, it was thought, by one of the Lords reviewing the case, Lord Bridge, that where a building remained a potential source of injury to persons or property on neighbouring land or on the highway, the owner ought in principle be able to recover in tort from the negligent builder any costs incurred in order to protect himself from potential liabilities to third parties.

Most significantly, the Lords attached weight to the fact that it is the claimant's knowledge of the defect which makes the defect one of quality only, and therefore the loss purely economic. However, such knowledge has not necessarily barred the right of recovery. One such case which highlighted this was *Rimmer v Liverpool City Council* (CA 1984). In this case, the designers and builders of a council flat, the local authority, was liable to a tenant injured by a pane of dangerously thin glass. The tenant knew of the danger and had complained, to no avail. It was considered that it was not practical for the tenant to either leave the flat or to change the pane of glass himself, although damages were reduced for contributory negligence.

Psychiatric illness

In *Alcock v Chief Constable of South Yorkshire* (HL 1991) Lord Ackner stated that shock "involves the sudden appreciation by sight or sound of a horrifying event, which violently agitates the mind".

Shock must manifest itself in some recognisable psychiatric or physical illness. Mere grief or emotional upset is not actionable, although mental distress suffered as a result of negligently inflicted injuries may be taken into account in the assessment of damages for pain and suffering.

Shock victims fall into two (very) broad groups, those who are unwilling participants in the events causing shock (known as primary victims) and those who are merely passive and unwilling victims (secondary victims). In relation to the first group, Lord Ackner said that if the defendants negligent conduct foreseeably puts the plaintiff in that position it follows that there will be a sufficiently proximate relationship between them, though if personal injury of some kind to the plaintiff is reasonably foreseeable as the result of an accident the defendant is liable for psychiatric injury (even though no physical injury occurs) and the plaintiff need not prove that injury by shock was foreseeable because the defendant must take his victim as he finds him.

Subsequent cases have established three types of primary victim, namely those who are put in reasonable fear for their own safety, rescuers and those who reasonably believe that they are about to be, or have been, the involuntary cause of another's death or injury. Such persons will recover if shock to them was reasonably foreseeable or if personal injury of some kind was foreseeable.

Where shock victims fall within the second category of groups a more complex analysis is required. It was held in Alcock that in order to recover damages, the plaintiff had to prove the following:

a) that his relationship to the primary victim was sufficiently close that it was reasonably foreseeable that he might suffer shock if he apprehended that the victim had been, or might be, injured;

b) that he was temporally and spatially close to the scene of the accident or its immediate aftermath;

c) that he suffered shock through sight or hearing of the accident or its immediate aftermath.

One matter not covered in Alcock was whether a plaintiff could recover for shock caused as a result of witnessing the destruction of property. In *Attia v British Gas plc* (CA 1988) it was held that there was no principle of law that shock in such circumstances could never be regarded as foreseeable. However, since the defendants in that case admitted to owing a duty in respect of the damage to the plaintiff's home, the shock issue was treated as one of remoteness rather than duty.

Omissions

In tort, as a general rule, the defendant does not owe a duty to take positive action to prevent harm to others. For example, the failure of a public authority to exercise a statutory power, or a statutory duty, will not normally give rise to a common law duty (see *Stovin v Wise* HL 1996). The mere existence of statutory powers and duties did not create a parallel common law duty. This was highlighted in the case of *Gorringe v Calderdale* (2004) where the highway authorities failure to paint a marking or to erect a road sign warning of a dangerous stretch of road did not give rise to a duty of care to the claimant.

Negligence-breach of duty

Once it has been established that a duty of care is owed to a claimant, it must then be proven that the defendant was in breach of that duty.

The key definition of negligence and duty of care was defined in *Blythe v Birmingham Waterworks* Co (1856). In this case, a wooden plug in a water main became loose in a severe frost. The plug led to a pipe which in turn went up the street. However, this pipe was blocked with ice, and the water instead flooded the claimant's house. The claimant sued in negligence. In this case, Alderson B defined negligence as:

"the omission to do something which a reasonable man, guided upon those considerations which ordinarily regulate the conduct of human affairs, would do, or doing something which a prudent and reasonable man would not do".
The key word here is "*reasonable man*". The standard of care required of the defendant is that of the hypothetical reasonable man. This standard is objective as it does not take into account particular traits of an individual. In *Hall v Brooklands Auto Racing Club* (1933) Greer LJ described such a person as:

- the 'man in the street'; or
- 'the man on the Clapham Omnibus; or

- 'the man who takes the magazines at home, and in the evening pushes the lawnmower in his shirt sleeves'

The reasonable person is therefore an 'average' person and not perfect.

The standard of reasonable care is invariable in the sense that the law does not recognise differing degrees of negligence but it is an infinitely flexible concept enabling the court in any given situation to impose standards ranging from high to low.

What is reasonable conduct varies with the particular circumstance, and liability depends ultimately what the reasonable man would have foreseen, which in turn may depend upon what particular knowledge and experience, if any, is to be attributed to him. However, although a defendant is not negligent if the consequences of his conduct were unforeseeable, it does not necessarily follow that the defendant will be responsible for all foreseeable consequences. In practice the courts evaluate a defendant's behaviour in terms of risk, so that he will be seen to be negligent if the claimant is exposed to an unreasonable risk of harm.

Special standards of care

There are certain situations in which the courts will apply a different standard of care from that of the 'reasonable' person:

- Where the defendant has a particular skill
- Where the defendant has a particular lack of skill
- Where the defendant is a child
- Where the defendant is competing in or watching a sporting event.

Skilled or professional defendants

The standard of care applied to professional with a particular skill or expertise is that of the reasonable person with the same skill or expertise. For example a doctor would be expected to show a greater degree of skill and care to a patient than 'the man on the Clapham omnibus'. See below.

Magnitude of the risk

The degree of care which the law expects must be commensurate with the risk created. Two factors are involved, namely the likelihood that harm will be caused and the potential gravity of that harm. In the case *Bolton v Stone* (HL 1951) the plaintiff was standing in the road when she was struck by a cricket ball which had been hit out of the defendants ground. There was some evidence that this had happened before on an infrequent basis, i.e. six times in thirty years, so that the risk was one of which the defendants were aware and which was reasonably foreseeable. However, the defendants were not held liable because the risk was so small that they were perfectly justified in not taking any further measures to eliminate that risk.

Another case illustrating magnitude and gravity of the risk is that of *Paris v Stepney B.C* (HL 1951) where a person with one eye, a garage worker, became totally blind after being struck in the eye by a metal chip which flew from a bolt which he was trying to hammer loose. The defendants, his employers, were held liable for failing to provide him with safety goggles, even though they were justified in not providing such equipment to a person with normal sight. Although the risk was small, the injury to this particular person was very serious.

Another case which illustrates the magnitude of risk is that of *Watson v British Boxing Board of Control* (2001) where the board breached its duty in failing to inform itself adequately about the risks inherent to a blow to the head and by failing to provide resuscitation equipment to be provided at the ringside together with persons able to operate it.

The degree of risk to which a claimant is exposed will also depend upon any physical abnormality from which he may suffer so that, if such abnormality is or ought to be known to the defendant, that is a factor which should be taken into account.

Characteristics of the defendant

The general legal standard does not take into account the personal characteristics of a particular defendant. Inexperience, lack of intelligence or other provide no defence to negligence. For example, a partially sighted driver owes the same level of duty as a normally sighted driver. However, two types of defendant require mention.

Evidence of negligence

It is for the claimant to prove, on a balance of probabilities, that the defendant was negligent. This is subject to the proviso contained within the Civil Evidence Act 1968 s.11, that proof that a person stands convicted of an offence is conclusive evidence in civil proceedings that he did commit it unless the contrary is proved. The effect of this provision is to shift the burden of proof where the claimant proves that the defendant has been convicted of an offence involving conduct complained of as negligent, such as careless driving.

In order to discharge the burden of proof the claimant must usually prove particular conduct on the part of the defendant which can be regarded as negligent. The claimant will not be able to do so, however, if he does not know how the accident was caused and, in such a case, the maxim *res ipsa loquitur* (the thing speaks for itself) may be relied on.

This is a rule of evidence that the claimant, who is unable to explain how the accident happened, asks the court to make a *prima facie* finding of negligence, which it is then for the defendant to rebut if he or she can. There are three conditions necessary for the application of the doctrine which arose out of *Scott v London and St Katherines Docks Co (EC 1865):* there must be an absence of an explanation as to how the accident happened, the 'thing' which causes the damage must be under control of the defendant (or someone for whose negligence he is responsible) and the accident must be such as would not ordinarily occur without negligence.

****

2.2

NEGLIGENCE-CAUSATION AND REMOTENESS OF DAMAGE

Causation

It must first be established that the breach was the cause of the damage, or materially contributed to the damage. In determining this issue, it is usual to employ the 'but for' test, the function of which is to eliminate those factors which could not have had any causal effect. One case which illustrates this is *Cork v Kirby Maclean 1952* Where a workman, an epileptic, was set to work painting the roof inside a factory, which necessitated his doing the work from a platform some 23 feet above the floor of the factory. The platform was some 27 inches wide and was used for the deposit of the workman's brush and bucket. There were no guard-rails or toe boards. The workman fell from the platform and was killed. In this case, Lord Denning stated:

...if the damage would not have happened but for a particular fault, then that fault is the cause of the damage; if it would have happened just the same, fault or no fault, the fault is not the cause of the damage.

Another case is *Barnett v Chelsea and Kensington Hospital Management Committee* (HC 1969) where the failure of a casualty officer to examine a patient, who subsequently died of arsenic poisoning, was held not to have been a cause of death because evidence showed that the patient would have probably died in any event.

Difficulties may arise where the precise cause of the damage is unknown. In *McGhee v National Coal Board* (HL 1972) the patient contracted dermatitis as a result of exposure to abrasive dust at work. His employers were not at fault for the exposure during the normal course of his work, but were found to be negligent for failing to provide washing facilities with the result that he was caked in dust for longer than necessary as he cycled home. The plaintiff succeeded on the ground that it was sufficient to show that the defendant's breach materially increased the risk of injury, even though medical knowledge at the time was unable to establish the breach as the probable cause. This decision had far reaching effects, particularly in cases of medical negligence.

An attempt was made in *Hotson v East Berkshire Area Health Authority* (HL 1987) to extend the principle so as to impose a liability in respect of the loss of a chance of recovery. In this case, the plaintiff injured his hip in a fall and, as a result of negligent medical diagnosis, suffered a permanent deformity the risk of which would have been reduced by 25 per cent had the proper treatment been given at the time. The Court of Appeal upheld the finding but this was overturned by the House of Lords on the grounds that there was no principle in law which would have justified a discount from the full measure of damages.

In cases where successive acts cause damage, the position is more complex. In *Baker v Willoughby* (HL 1970) the plaintiff's leg was injured through the defendant's negligence, and some time later, before the trial, he was shot in the same leg during a robbery. The leg was then amputated. It was held in this case that the plaintiff's right of recovery was not limited to the loss suffered only before the date of the robbery, but that he was entitled to damages that he would have received had there been no subsequent injury.

In another case, *Jobling v Associated Dairies Limited* (HL 1980) the defendant's negligence caused a reduction in the plaintiffs earning capacity. Three years later, but before the trial, the defendant was found to be suffering from another complaint, wholly unrelated to the original accident, which totally incapacitated him. The defendant's were held liable only for the loss up to the time of the plaintiff's disablement.

Remoteness of damage

The plaintiff is not entitled to compensation for every consequence of the defendant's wrong. In order to contain the defendant's liability within reasonable bounds, a line is drawn, and the consequences that fall on the far side of the line are said to be too remote and not having been caused in law by the defendant's breach of duty.

There are a number of cases which have provided tests of remoteness of damage. In *Re Polemis and Furness, Withy and Co* (CA 1921) a ship's cargo of benzene had leaked filling the hold with inflammable vapour. Stevedores unloading the vessel negligently dropped a plank in the hold, and the defendant employers were held liable for the destruction of the ship in the blaze that followed because that loss was a direct, although unforeseeable consequence of the negligence.

Whilst not denying the relevance of foreseeability to the existence of a duty, the case did decide that it was not relevant in determining for what consequences the defendant should pay.

However, in another case, *Overseas Tankship (UK) Ltd v Morts Dock Engineering Co Ltd* (*The Wagon Mound*), 1961 this approach was disproved. A test of reasonable foresight of consequence was substituted for that of directness. The defendants, in this case, negligently discharged into Sydney Harbour a large quantity of fuel oil which drifted to the plaintiff's wharf whilst welding was in progress. The plaintiff's discontinued their operations, but later resumed following an assurance that there was no danger of the oil igniting. A fire did eventually break out, causing damage to the wharf and to two ships upon which work was being carried out. It was found as a fact that some damage to the wharf was reasonably foreseeable by way of fouling the slipway, but that, in view of expert evidence, it was unforeseeable that the oil would ignite. The defendant's were, accordingly, held not liable.

Manner of occurrence

In *Hughes v Lord Advocate* (HL 1963) post office employees negligently left a manhole uncovered with a canvas shelter over it, surrounded by paraffin lamps. The plaintiff, aged eight, took none of the lamps into the shelter and knocked it into the manhole. There was an explosion, following an unusual combination of circumstances, in which the boy was badly burned. Although the explosion was unforeseeable, the defendants were held liable because burns from the lamp were foreseeable, and it was immaterial that the precise chain of events leading to the injury was not.

A contrasting case is that of *Doughty v Turner Manufacturing Co Ltd* (CA 1964) in which the defendant's employee dropped an asbestos cover into a vat of molten liquid which, due to an unforeseeable chemical reaction, erupted and burned a fellow worker standing nearby. It was held that, even if injury by splashing were foreseeable the eruption was not, and the plaintiff failed. This case is at odds with Hughes (above) because if it accepted that some injury by burning was foreseeable, then it ought not to matter that the way in which it occurred was not.

Type of damage

The exact nature of the damage need not be foreseeable, provided it is of a type that could have been foreseen. The difficulty here, of defining damage 'of a type' is illustrated by two contrasting cases. The first case, *Bradford v Robinson Rentals Ltd* (HC 1967) a van driver sent on a long journey in an unheated vehicle in severe weather was able to recover damages for frostbite because, although not in itself foreseeable, it was in the broad class of foreseeable risk arising from exposure to severe cold.

The second case, *Tremain v Pike* (HC 1969) the defendant's alleged negligence caused his farm to become rat-infested with the result that the plaintiff contracted a rare disease by contact with rats urine. It was held that, even if negligence had been proved, the plaintiff could not succeed because although injury from rat bites or food contamination was foreseeable, this particularly rare disease was entirely different in kind.

Extent of damage

When considering the extent of damage, it doesn't matter that the actual damage is far greater in extent than could have been foreseen. In *Vacwell Engineering Co Ltd v B.D.H. Chemicals Ltd* (CA 1971) the plaintiffs purchased a chemical manufactured and supplied by the defendants, who failed to give warning that it was liable to cause a minor explosion on contact with water. The plaintiff's employee placed a large amount of the chemical in a sink and an explosion of unforeseeable violence badly damaged the premises. Since the explosion and subsequent damage were foreseeable, even though the extent was not, the defendants were held liable.

A similar rule operates where the claimant suffers foreseeable personal injury which is exacerbated by some pre-existing physical or psychic abnormality. This so called "egg-shell skull" principle imposes liability on the defendant for harm which is not only greater in extent than, but which is of an entirely different kind to, that which is foreseeable. In *Smith v Leech Brain and Co Ltd* (HC 1962) a workman who had a predisposition to cancer received a burn on the lip from molten metal due to a colleague's negligence. The defendants were held liable for his subsequent death from cancer triggered by the burn.

The principle applies equally to a claimant who suffers from nervous shock. In *Meah v McCreamer* (HC 1985) the plaintiff underwent a marked personality change brought about by injuries received in a collision for which the defendant was responsible. This led him to commit a series of assaults for which he received a life sentence. He recovered damages for loss of liberty.

Intervening causes

In some cases, the claimant's damage is alleged to be attributable not to the defendant's breach of duty, but to some intervening event which breaks the chain of causation. Such an event is called a *novus actus interveniens* and is usually dealt with as part of the issue of remoteness because even though the damage would not have occurred "but for" the defendants breach, it may still be regarded in law as falling outside the scope of the risk created by the original fault. One such case that illustrates this is *McKew v Holland* and *Hannen and Cubitts* (Scotland) Ltd (HL 1969) where the plaintiff's leg occasionally gave way without warning as a result of the defendant's negligence. On one such occasion he fractured his ankle as a result of descending a flight of stairs where his leg gave way.

The defendant's were held not liable for this further injury because, although foreseeable, the plaintiff's conduct was *so* unreasonable as to amount to a *novus actus*. However, each case on its own merit. Whether the issue is seen as *novus actus* or of contributory negligence (which is the more common approach) will depend upon the nature of the plaintiff's conduct and it may be that a positive act is more likely to break the causal chain than a mere omission.

Intervention of a third party

According to Lord Reid in *Dorset Yacht Co Ltd v Home Office* (HL 1970) the intervention of a third party must have been something very likely to happen if it is not regarded as breaking the chain of causation. The question is what is the potential liability of a defendant for the criminal act of another? In the case *Knightly v Johns* (CA 1982) the defendant negligently caused a crash on a dangerous bend in a one-way tunnel. The police inspector at the scene of the accident forgot to close the tunnel to oncoming traffic as he ought to have done in accordance with standing orders, so he ordered the plaintiff officer to ride back on his motorcycle against the flow of traffic in order to do so, and the plaintiff was injured in a further collision. It was said that, in considering whether the intervening act of a third party breaks the chain of causation, the test is whether the damage is reasonably foreseeable in the sense of being a 'natural and probable' result of the defendant's breach. A deliberate decision to do a positive act is more likely to break the chain than a mere omission. In this case, the inspector's errors amounted to tortuous negligence which cannot be described as the natural and probable consequence of the original collision, and the defendant was held not liable.

Intervening natural force

The defendant will not normally be held liable for damage suffered as the immediate consequence of a natural event which occurs independently of the breach. In the case *Carslogie Steamship Co Ltd v Royal Norwegian Government* (HL 1952) the defendants were held not liable for storm damage suffered by a ship during a voyage to a place where repairs to collision damage caused by the defendant's negligence were to be done, even though that voyage would not have been undertaken had the collision not occurred.

Contributory Negligence

Since the passage of the Law Reform (Contributory Negligence) Act 1945 contributory negligence is no longer a complete bar to recovery but, in accordance with s.1(1) of the act, will result in a reduction of damages to such an extent as is seen as just and equitable.

The Act applies where the damage is attributable to the fault of both parties, and 'fault' is defined in section 4 to mean "negligence, breach of statutory duty, or other act or omission which gives rise to a liability in tort or would, apart from this act, give rise to the defence of contributory negligence". The defence, therefore, applies to actions other than negligence, though it does not apply to deceit or intentional interference with goods - Torts (Interference With Goods) Act 1977 s.11).

Causation

The damage suffered must be caused partly by the fault of the claimant and it is therefore irrelevant that the claimant's fault was nothing to do with the accident. Thus, reductions in damages have been made for failure to wear a seat belt or a crash helmet and for travelling in a vehicle with a drunk driver.

One case which highlights this is *Jones v Livox Quarries Ltd (CA 1952)*. The plaintiff, contrary to instructions, stood on a rear towbar of a vehicle and was injured when another vehicle ran into the back of it. In this case, damages were reduced as the claimant had exposed himself to risk. The claimant is expected to show an objective standard of care in much the same way as the defendant must to avoid tortuous negligence.

There are particular cases in contributory negligence, children, old or infirm persons and rescuers merit special attention.

Children

As a matter of law thee is no age below which it can be said that a child is incapable of contributory negligence. However, the degree of care expected must be apportioned to the age of the child. For example, in *Gough v Thorne (CA 1966)* a 13 year old girl who was knocked down by a negligent motorist when she stepped past a stationary lorry whose driver had beckoned her to cross, was held not guilty of contributory negligence. However, in *Morales v Eccleston* (CA 1991) an 11 year old boy who was struck by the defendant driver while kicking a ball in the middle of the road with traffic passing in either direction had his damages reduced by 75 per cent.

Old or infirm persons

When assessing whether such a person is guilty of contributory negligence, the age and infirmity and its impact on the alleged negligence is taken into account.

Rescuers

It is not very often, for obvious reasons, that a rescuer will be found guilty of contributory negligence. In *Brandon v Osborne, Garret and Co Ltd* (HC 1924) the defendants negligently allowed a sheet of glass to fall from their shop roof and the plaintiff, believing her husband to be in danger, tried to pull him away and injured her leg. She was held to not be contributorily negligent. A similar principle applies where the claimant is injured in trying to extricate himself or herself from a perilous situation in which the defendants negligence has placed them, even though, with hindsight the claimant is shown to have chosen the wrong course of action. As with all such cases, each case is viewed on its own merit.

Apportionment

Apportionment is on a just and equitable basis according to the 1945 Act and, in assessing the claimant's reduction, the court may take into account both the potency of his act and the degree of blameworthiness to be attached to it. The Court of Appeal has held, in *Johnson v Tennant Bros Ltd* (CA 1954) that no apportionment should be made unless one of the parties is at least 10 per cent to blame. However, the decisions concerning apportionment is left, mainly, to judicial discretion.

Violenti Non Fit Injuria

This maxim embodies a principle that a person who expressly or impliedly agrees with another to run the risk of harm created by that other person cannot then sue in respect of damage suffered as a result of the materialisation of that risk. The defence is called consent or voluntary assumption of risk and, if successful, is a complete bar to recovery.

For the defence to apply the defendant must have committed what would, in the absence of any consent, amount to a tort. The defendant must prove not only that the claimant consented to the risk of actual damage, but also that he or she agreed to waive their right of action in respect of that damage.

Knowledge of the risk

Knowledge of the risk does not amount to consent. It must be found that the claimant, with full knowledge of the risk, agreed to incur it.

Agreement

In relation to agreement, in addition to the claimant being willing to take the risk, there must be evidence that the claimant has expressly or impliedly agreed to waive his or her course of action. An express antecedent agreement to relieve the defendant of liability for future negligence operates in effect as an exclusion notice and is therefore subject to the Unfair Contract terms Act 1977. Section 2(1) renders void any purported exclusion of liability for death or personal injury caused by negligence and, in the case of other loss or damage, s.2(2) subjects such an exclusion to a test of reasonableness. Section 2(3) further provides that a persons agreement to, or awareness of, such a notice is not of itself to be taken as indicating his voluntary acceptance of any risk. These provisions only apply to business liability.

In some circumstances the conduct of the parties may enable an inference to be drawn that the claimant has impliedly agreed to waive his legal rights in respect of future negligence. One such case was *Morris v Murray* (CA 1990). The defence applied when, in poor weather conditions, the defendant, who to the plaintiff's knowledge was extremely drunk, took the plaintiff for a spin and crashed the aircraft immediately after takeoff.

With negligence cases in the sporting arena, the potential liability of the participant depends upon the standard of care owed. In any sporting event, the spectator may be taken to have accepted the risks incidental to the game, for example, being hit by a cricket ball whilst watching a game of cricket. In the case *Wooldridge v Sumner* (CA 1963) it was stated that sportsmen and women have a duty not to behave with reckless disregard for the spectator. This applies to the duty of care required between one player and another. In *Watson v British Boxing Board of Control* (2001) it was pointed out that where the plaintiff consents to injury by an opponent in a boxing ring he does not consent to injury resulting from inadequate safety arrangements by the sports governing body after being hit.

Ex Turpi Causa

Where an alleged wrong occurs whilst the claimant is engaged in criminal activity, the claim may be barred because ex *turpi causa non oritur actio (no action can be founded on an illegal act)*. This principle is based on public policy and may also apply where the claimant's conduct is immoral. The difficulty is deciding which types of conduct are considered sufficiently heinous for the purposes of defence. Some cases have found that it will apply where it would be impossible to determine an appropriate standard of care, whilst others have suggested that the claimant ought not to succeed if to permit him to do so would be an affront to the public conscience.

In *Clunis v Camden and Islington Health Authority* (CA 1998) the plaintiff, who had a long history of mental illness, was convicted of manslaughter and ordered to be detained in a secure hospital. He sued the defendant for negligence for failing to take reasonable care to provide him with after care services following his discharge from hospital where he had been detained under the Mental Health Act 1983.

It was held that, despite a successful plea of diminished responsibility at the criminal trial, his action was barred on the grounds of public policy since he was directly implicated in the illegality and must be taken to have known that what he was doing was wrong.

In *Vellino v Chief Constable of Greater Manchester Police* (CA 2001) the claimant suffered brain damage when he attempted to escape from police custody by jumping though a window on the second floor. Negligence was claimed on the part of the arresting officers, alleging that they had stood by and let him jump. The Court of Appeal held that the claim was untenable because the defendant had to rely on his own criminal conduct in escaping lawful custody to found his claim.

****

2.3

NEGLIGENCE-EMPLOYERS LIABILITY

In addition to common law duty, there is a large body of statutory obligations which the employer has to abide by when protecting its workforce. In relation to accidents and other forms of negligence it is common for employers to sue both in negligence and breach of statutory duty. Employers have a statutory duty to insure against liability, as laid down by the Employers Liability (Compulsory Insurance) Act 1969.

Nature of the duty

Although there once existed the doctrine of common employment, in which there was an implied term in a contract of employment that employees accepted risks incidental to their employment, the law has changed significantly.

The doctrine of common employment was abolished in 1948 and, as the law has evolved, employers have a personal duty and a vicarious liability towards their employees. Traditionally, the duty is said to be threefold, which was highlighted in the case of *Wilsons and Clyde Coal Co Ltd v English* (HL 1938), namely "the provision of a competent staff of men, adequate material and a proper system and effective supervision". The duty is not absolute but is discharged by the exercise of reasonable care and is thus similar to the duty of care in the tort of negligence generally. Although most of the cases concern work accidents, the duty extends to guarding against disease and gradual deterioration in health as a result of adverse working conditions. This was illustrated in the case of *Thompson v Smith's Ship repairers (North Shields) Ltd* (HC 1984). However, it does not extend to the prevention of economic loss by, for example, advising the employee to take out insurance nor the prevention of injury to health caused by self-induced intoxication.

Safe plant and equipment

The employer has a duty to take reasonable care to provide proper plant and equipment and to maintain them so as to keep them in good order. This includes the provision of protective devices and clothing appropriate to the job, and also a warning or exhortation from the employer to make use of such equipment.

One case which highlights this is *Bux v Slough Metals Ltd* (CA 1973) where the plaintiff, a foundry worker, lost the sight of one eye when splashed with molten metal. Although the employer had, in compliance with statutory regulations, provided protective goggles, he was held liable for breach of his common law duty, which extended to persuading and even insisting on the use of protective equipment. Most employees will now be protected by the Personal Protective Equipment at Work Regulations 1992, which impose a statutory duty to take all reasonable steps to see that protective equipment is properly used, though it is the employee's duty to use it.

In relation to injury caused by defective equipment, in the case *Davie v New Merton Board Mills Ltd* (HL 1959) it was held that the duty to provide proper tools was satisfied by purchase from a reputable supplier. This decision has now been reversed however, by the Employer's Liability (Defective Equipment) Act 1969, which renders an employer personally liable in negligence if two conditions are met: first, that the employee is injured in the course of his employment by a defect in equipment issued by the employer for the purposes of the employer's business and, secondly, that the defect is attributable wholly or partly to the fault of a third party, (whether identifiable or not. Such a third party could be the manufacturer. Strict liability is thus imposed upon the employer if his employee can prove that some third party was at fault, though contributory negligence can be used as a defence by that third party.

The employee might also be able to rely on the Provision and Use of Work Equipment Regulations 1992 which provide that employers must ensure that work equipment is so constructed or adapted as to be suitable for the purpose for which it is to be used or provided, and that such equipment is maintained in an efficient state.

Safe system of work

A safe system of work means the organisation of work, the manner in which it is to be carried out, the organising and planning of numbers of men and women and their tasks and the instructions given to these workers. One case illustrating this is *Johnstone v Bloomsbury Health Authority* (CA 1991) where it was held that requiring the plaintiff to work such long hours as might foreseeably injure his health could constitute a breach of duty. In *Walker v Nortumberland County Council* (HC 1995) the plaintiff suffered a nervous breakdown as a result of work pressure. Before returning to work it was agreed that assistance would be provided to reduce his workload. Very little was actually provided and he suffered a second breakdown which forced him to stop work permanently. His employers were held liable for failing to provide a safe place of work in that they continued to employ him without adequate assistance. In *Waters v Commissioner of Police of the Metropolis* (2000) the House of Lords held that an employer is under a duty to take reasonable care to protect its employees from harm, including workplace bullying and psychiatric harm, where the employer knows or can foresee that an employee might suffer this harm through the acts of fellow employees.

In *Hatton v Sutherland* (2002) the Court of Appeal ruled that claims for stress induced psychiatric illness follow the standard principles governing personal injury claims in that no special control mechanisms are applied to claims for psychiatric or physical injury arising from stress at work. The ordinary principles of employer's liability apply and the questions to be determined are:

- was there a breach of employer's duty of care which caused psychiatric harm to the employee?
- Was the psychiatric harm to that particular employee reasonably foreseeable?

The duty of care does not arise where the employer is unaware of the employee's vulnerability to stress induced illness or of an imminent psychiatric breakdown.

Safe premises

The employer's obligation includes making the premises as safe as possible. However, the employer is not required to eliminate every foreseeable risk if the burden in so doing is too onerous. In *Wilson v Tyneside Window Cleaning* (CA 1958) where it was held that the duty exists equally in relation to premises in the occupation or control of the third party. In appropriate circumstances an employer must be expected to go and inspect the premises to see that they are reasonably safe for the work to be carried out on them. However, the fact that the employer does not have control of the workplace is important in determining whether he has been negligent. Most workplaces are now governed by the Workplace (Health, Safety and Welfare) Regulations 1992.

Scope of the duty

The scope of the duty relates to the employer-employee and does not extend to an independent contractor. The duty is personal and non-delegable, so that the employer does not discharge his duty by entrusting its performance to another, whether that be an employer or independent contractor.

VICARIOUS LIABILITY

The employer-employee relationship is the most common example of vicarious liability. The negligence committed by an employee can thus ultimately be the liability of the employer.

OCCUPIERS LIABILITY

The occupier of a property in respect of loss or injury suffered by those who enter a property or its grounds lawfully is governed by the Occupiers Liability Act 1957. prior to this Act, the extent of liability owed by an occupier depended upon the relationship with the person injured. The OLA 1957 abolished this in favour of two categories:

- Lawful visitors, who were protected by the Act
- All others who were not protected

This Act was supplemented by the Occupiers Liability Act 1984 which covers injuries to trespassers.

Section 2(1) of the 1957 Act provides:

"An occupier owes the same duty, the 'common duty of care' to all his visitors, except in so far as he is free to, and does extend, restrict, modify or exclude his duty to any visitor or visitors by agreement or otherwise".

Who is an occupier?

The Act contains no clear definition of an "occupier". This is simply a term to denote a person who has a sufficient degree of control over premises to put him under a duty of care towards those who lawfully come on to the premises. Control is the decisive factor and it is not material that the occupier has no interest in the land, he could be tenant, lessee, licensee or any other person having the right to possession. One case illustrating this is *AMF International Ltd v Magnet Bowling Ltd* (HC 1968) where building contractors were held to be joint occupiers along with the building owners. A landlord who has let his property to a tenant will not be the occupier of the demised parts but will still be held to be the occupier of those parts, i.e. common parts, not demised to the tenant.

The premises

The definition of premises is wide and covers not only land and buildings. By s.1 (3)(a) of the Act, the statutory provisions extend to any fixed or moveable structure, including any vessel, vehicle or aircraft. This is apt to include not only structures of a permanent nature but also temporary structures such as ladders and scaffolding.

Visitors

The statutory duty is owed only to visitors who, by s.1 (2) are those who would, at common law, have been either invitees or licensees. For a licence to have been inferred there must be evidence that the occupier has permitted entry as opposed to merely tolerating it, as there is no positive obligation to keep the trespasser out. Repeated trespass of itself confers no licence. However, in some cases the courts have gone to great lengths to infer the existence of a licence. One case illustrating this is *Lowery v Walker* (HL 1911) where members of the public had for many years used the defendant's field as a short cut to the railway station. The defendant had often prevented them from so doing but did nothing further to stop them until, without warning, he turned a savage horse loose in the field. The animal attacked and injured the plaintiff who then sued and succeeded in his action on the basis that he was a licensee not a trespasser.

There are a number of other types of entrant that must be considered. Those who enter premises for any purpose in the exercise of a right conferred by law are treated, by s.2(6) of the Act as having the occupiers permission to be there for that purpose (whether they have it or not). Secondly, s.5(1) provides that where a person enters under the terms of a contract with the occupier there is, in the absence of express provision in the contract, an implied term that the entrant is owed the common duty of care and, according to *Sole v W.J Hallt Ltd* (HC 1973) he may frame his claim either in contract or under the 1957 Act. It is further provided by s.3(1) that where a person contracts with the occupier on the basis that a third party is to have access to the premises, the duty owed by the occupier to such third party as his visitor cannot be reduced by the terms of the contract to a level lower than the common duty of care. Conversely, if the contract imposes upon the occupier any obligation which exceeds the requirements of the statutory duty, then the third party is entitled to the benefit of that additional obligation.

Thirdly, those who use public or private rights of way are not visitors for the purposes of the 1957 Act, though the user of a private right of way is now owed a duty under the Occupiers Liability Act 1984 (see later).

Exclusions

As has been outlined, the duty owed to a contractual entrant is governed by the terms of the contract and a person who enters under a contract to which he is not party is, at the very least, owed a duty of care. In the case of no-contractual entrants, it is clear that, at common law, an occupier may be able to exclude or limit his liability by notice, provided that reasonable steps are taken to bring it to the visitor's attention and that the notice is clear and not misleading in any way. One case that illustrates this is *Ashdown v Samuel Williams and Sons* (CA 1956) where it was held that the plaintiff, who was injured by the negligent shunting of a railway wagon upon the defendants premises, was defeated in her claim by exclusion notices erected by the defendant saying that person entered at their own risk and no liability would be accepted for loss or damage, whether caused by negligence or otherwise.

The basic principle is that if an occupier can prevent people from entering his premises, then he can equally impose conditions, subject to which entry is permitted. However, the power of the occupier to exclude or restrict his liability for death or injury has been severely reduced by s.2 of the Unfair Contract Terms Act 1977. This section provides that a person cannot, by reference to a contract term or to a notice, exclude or restrict his liability for death or personal injury caused by negligence unless the term or contents of the notice satisfies the requirement of reasonableness.

The operations of s.2 of the Act is confined to those situations where there is business liability which is defined in s.1(3) as liability for breach of duty arising from things done in the course of a business or from the occupation of premises used for the business purposes of the occupier.

Common duty of care

The common duty of care is defined in s.2 (2) as:

"a duty to take such care as in all circumstances is reasonable to see that the visitor will be reasonably safe in using the premises for the purposes for which he is invited or permitted to be there"

This is similar to the common duty of care and may extend to taking steps to see that a visitor does not deliberately harm other visitors by foreseeably likely conduct. Whether the occupier has charged it depends on the facts, taking into account such matters as the nature of the danger, the purpose of the visit and the knowledge of the parties. In particular, there is provision in the act for Children, those with special skills, warning notices and independent contractors.

Children

The Act provides that the amount of care which an occupier can expect from a visitor will depend on certain factors. By s.2(3)(a) the occupier must be prepared for children to be less careful than an adult. However, case law has sought to balance responsibility between occupiers and parents.

The level of care expected will depend on the nature of the risk and the age and awareness of the child. For example, in the case *Titchener v BRB* 1983 no duty was owed to a 15 year old boy who was struck by a train whilst walking on a railway line at night as he was aware of the dangers posed by his activity.

Special skills

Section 2(3)(b) provides that:

"an occupier may expect that a person, in the exercise of his calling, will appreciate and guard against any special risks ordinarily incident to it, so far as the occupier leaves him free to do so".

In the case *Roles v Nathan* (CA 1963) the defendant was held not liable for the death of two chimney sweeps killed by carbon monoxide fumes while sealing up a flue in the defendant's boiler. If the same people had fallen through the floor because of a rotten floorboard the position would have been different.

Warnings

The occupier may, in accordance with s.2(4)(a) of the Act, discharge his duty by warning his visitor of the particular danger, provided that the notice is effective and the warning is sufficient to ensure that the visitor is reasonably safe. Warning notices have to be distinguished from exclusion notices. By sufficient warning the occupier discharges his duty, whereas exclusion purports to take away the right of recovery in respect of a breach. To be effective a warning must sufficiently identify the source of the danger.

Independent contractors

Where a visitor suffers damage due to faulty construction, maintenance or repair work by an independent contractor employed by the occupier, s 2 (4)(b) provides that the occupier will not be liable if it was reasonable to entrust the work to a contractor and he took such steps as he reasonably ought to see that the contractor was competent and had done the work properly. The occupier is not necessarily expected to check work of a technical nature although in the case of a complex project he may be under a duty to have the contractor's work supervised by a qualified specialist such as an architect or surveyor.

Defences

The provisions of the Law Reform (Contributory Negligence) Act 1945 apply and s.2(5) of the 1957 Act provides that an occupier is not liable in respect of risks which the visitor willingly accepts, thus allowing for the defence of *volenti non fit inujuria.* However, where there is business liability within the meaning of the Unfair Contract Terms Act 1977, s.2(3) of that Act provides that a person's agreement to or awareness of a notice purporting to exclude liability for negligence is not of itself to be taken as indicating his voluntary acceptance of the risk.

The Occupiers Liability Act 1984

The 1984 OLA extended the protection of the law to cover:

- Trespassers
- People lawfully exercising rights of way

- Visitors to land covered by section 60 of the National Parks and Access to the Countryside Act 1949 and 'right to room' legislation.

The 1984 Occupiers Liability Act governs the liability of an occupier to "persons other than his visitors" in respect of injury suffered by them on the premises due to the state of the premises or to things done or needing to be done to them. The term "persons other than his visitors" includes trespassers and persons exercising private rights of way, but those using public rights of way.

The scope of the duty

Section 1(3) of the 1984 Act provides that the occupier owes a duty if:

a) he is aware of the danger or has reasonable grounds to believe that it exists;

b) he knows or has reasonable grounds to believe that the non visitor is in the vicinity of the danger concerned or that he may come into the vicinity of the danger; and

c) the risk is one against which, in all the circumstances of the case, he may be reasonably expected to offer the non-visitor some protection.

Whilst paragraph (c) clearly adopts an objective test, paragraphs (a) and (b) import a subjective element in that the existence of a duty depends upon the occupiers actual knowledge of facts which should lead him to conclude that a danger exists. If the occupier is not aware of these facts he may not owe a duty.

In the case *Rhind v Astbury* (2004) the claimant accepted that he was a trespasser when he dived into shallow water to retrieve a football, but he argued that his injury was caused by a fibreglass container on the bed of the lake which constituted a danger within the meaning of s.1 (3) of the 1984 Act. The Court of Appeal held that the claimant had failed to establish a duty of care under s.1(3) since the defendant was unaware of the existence of the container and had no reasonable grounds for suspecting that the danger existed.

It is to be noted that the statutory duty applies only to personal injury or death. Liability for loss of, or damage to, property is expressly excluded by s. 1(8).

Defences

Section 1(5) of the Act provides that the occupier may, in appropriate cases, discharge his duty by taking reasonable steps to warn of the danger or to discourage persons from incurring the risk. Whether a warning is effective will depend among other things upon the nature of the risk and the age of the entrant.

The defence of *volenti non fit injuria* is preserved by s.1(6) of the Act. It is normally limited to dangers arising from the state of the premises. The plaintiff was held to have willingly accepted the risk as his own, within the meaning of s.1(6) of the Act in the case of *Rathcliffe v McDonnell* (CA 1999). In this case, the plaintiff, having drunk four pints agreed to go open-air swimming with his friends. He climbed over the gate of a college swimming pool. Although conscious of a warning sign he dived in the pool and suffered horrific injuries as a result.

The Court of Appeal rejected his claim for damages on the grounds that he was aware of the risk and had willingly accepted it.

As far as the defence of *ex turpi* is concerned, it was held in *Revill v Newberry* (CA 1996) that the fact that the plaintiff was a burglar did not take him outside the protection of the law, so that he was entitled to succeed in negligence when the defendant unintentionally shot him. There was, unsurprisingly, a substantial reduction in damages for contributory negligence.

Exclusion notices

There is no mention in the Act of excluding liability to the non-visitor, and the provisions of the Unfair Contract Terms Act 1977 do not apply to the 1984 duty. Trespassers pose problems because depending upon the point at which they enter the premises, they may be less likely to see a notice than a lawful visitor.

One suggested solution is that the duty under the 1984 Act is a minimum which cannot be excluded so that even the lawful visitor would be protected by it, even though he was aware of an exclusion notice.

Independent contractors and trespassers

At common law, the liability of a contractor to the trespasser rests upon ordinary negligence principles. The fact that the claimant is a trespasser in relation to the occupier is not relevant except in so far as the trespassers presence may be less foreseeable. One case which illustrates this is *Buckland v Guildford Gas Light and Coke Co* (HC 1949). The defendants, who had erected electricity cables on a farmer's land close to the top of a tree, were held liable for the death of a young girl who climbed the tree and was electrocuted.

Breach of statutory duty

Breach by the defendant of an obligation under statute (other than one which expressly seeks to impose liability in tort) may, apart from giving rise to any criminal sanction laid down in the Act, also enable a person injured by the breach to bring a civil action for damages for breach of statutory duty. This is a tort in its own right independent of any other form of tortuous liability. Whether a claimant can sue depends on whether the statute confers a right of civil action, or can be interpreted as conferring this right.

The claimant must prove that the legislature intended to create a right to sue. In *Cullen v Chief Constable of the Royal Ulster Constabulary* (2003) the House of Lords upheld the previous decisions that the claimant could not rely on the tort of breach of statutory duty for the failure of the police to give him reasons for delaying his access to a solicitor, on the ground that the duty concerned could be enforced through judicial review. In a few instances, Parliament has expressly made known its intention, but in the majority of cases statute is silent on the issue. It is for the courts to decide what the intention of an Act is and, to this end, certain guidelines have been established. The basic proposition is that a breach of statutory duty does not, by itself, give rise to a private law action. Such an action will arise, however, if it can be shown that, on the proper construction of the statute, the duty was imposed for the protection of a limited class of the public and Parliament intended to confer upon members of that class a right to sue for breach. There is no general rule for determining whether the Act does create such a right, but if no other remedy is provided for its breach that is an indicator in the claimant's favour. If the Act does contain other provision for enforcing the duty that is an indication of an intention that it was to be enforced by those means alone and not by private law action.

In determining whether, in any particular case, a civil action for breach of statutory duty will lie, the starting point is to look at precedent or for a clearly stated Parliamentary intention. In the absence of either it is in all cases a question of ascertaining the fundamental purpose the legislation intended to achieve, and that can only be done through a consideration of the Act as a whole.

The elements of the tort
Duty owed to the claimant
In establishing that breach of the particular duty will, in principle, ground a right of action, the claimant will, in most cases, have established that the obligation was imposed for the benefit of a limited class. The claimant must then prove that he is a member of that class.

In the case *Hartley v Mayoh and Co* (CA 1954) the widow of a fireman electrocuted while fighting a fire at the defendant's factory had no cause of action because the regulations existed for the benefit of "persons employed" and her husband was not so employed.

Defendant and breach of duty
The claimant must prove that the claimant was in breach. This can only be ascertained by having regard to the precise wording of the Act to determine the nature of the obligation. Some obligations are absolute, such as those contained within health and safety Acts.

Damage of the contemplated type
For the claimant to succeed the harm suffered must be of a type which the act

was designed to prevent. In the case, *Gorris v Scott* (1874) the plaintiffs sheep were swept overboard the defendant's vessel during a storm. The sheep were not penned, contrary to statutory regulations, but the plaintiff failed in his action because the object of the regulations was to prevent the spread of disease, not to afford protection from the dangers of the sea.

Another case illustrating this is *Donaghey v Boulton and Paul Limited* (HL 1968) where the plaintiff slipped and fell through an open space in an asbestos roof on which he was working. In breach of their duty the defendants had failed to provide him with adequate crawling boards, but argued that the object of the regulations was to prevent workers from falling through fragile roofing materials, not through holes in the roof. This argument was rejected and the House of Lords held the defendant's liable.

Causation

The burden rests upon the claimant to prove on a balance of probabilities that the breach of statutory duty caused or materially contributed to the damage. In this respect there is no distinction between this tort and a common law negligence action, so that the claimant must show that he would not have been injury were it not for the defendant's breach. The claimant must also show that the damage is not too remote and the usual test of reasonable foresight applies.

A problem arises where the claimant's own wrongful act puts the defendant in breach. In *Ginty v Belmont Building Supplies Ltd* (HC 1959) a regulation binding upon both parties required the use of crawling boards on a fragile roof. The defendant had provided the boards and given full instructions to the plaintiff how to use them. The plaintiff neglected to use them and fell through the roof. Both parties were clearly in breach of their statutory obligation but it was held that the plaintiff was the sole cause of his injury and his action failed.

Even if the claimant is in breach of his statutory duty he will fail in his action if it is his own deliberate folly which puts the defendant in breach. However, this will be mitigated by the actions of the defendant if he is also in breach.

112

2.4

NEGLIGENCE-LIABILITY FOR DANGEROUS/DEFECTIVE PRODUCTS

Part 1 of the Consumer Protection Act 1987, which came into force on 1ˢᵗ March 1988, creates a strict liability for dangerous goods.

Part 1 was enacted to give effect to an E.C. Directive of 1985, requiring the harmonisation of law on product liability throughout the E.C. If the Act doesn't apply in certain circumstances a claimant may still be able to sue for negligence. When claiming damages for harm suffered as a result of a defective product, the claimant must prove that he or she suffered damage caused wholly or partly by a defect arising from a specific product.

The Act (s.2.(2)) outlines who the potential defendants might be in such cases:

a) the producer of the product;
b) any person who holds himself out to be a producer by putting his name or trade mark or any other distinguishing mark on the product;
c) an importer of the product into a Member State from a place outside the E.C. in order to supply it to another in the course of his business.

The term 'producer' is defined in s.1(2) to mean either the manufacturer, or the person who won or extracted the product, or, where the product has not been manufactured, won or abstracted but the essential characteristics of which are attributable to an industrial or other process having been carried out, the person who carried out that process.

Furthermore, by s.2(3) the mere supplier (e.g. Retailer) is liable if he fails within a reasonable time to comply with the plaintiff's request to identify one or more of the persons to whom s.2(2) applies, or to identify his own supplier.

'Product' is defined in s.1(2) as any goods or electricity. Component parts and raw materials also fall within the definition of product as distinct from the overall product in which they are comprised. For example, the brakes in a car would be the responsibility of both manufacturer of brakes and the supplier of the finished car.

The meaning of 'defect'

A product is defective, according to s.3(1) if its safety is not such as persons are generally entitled to expect. The safety of a product expressly includes safety "with respect to products comprised within that product" (i.e. components and raw materials) and a product may be unsafe not only if there is a risk of personal injury but also if it poses a risk of damage to property. When determining what people are entitled to expect, s.3(2) provides that account shall be taken of all the circumstances including the following specific matters:

a) the way in which and the purposes for which the product has been marketed, its get-up, and warnings and instructions for use accompanying it:

b) what might reasonably be expected to be done with or in relation to the product;

c) the time when the product was supplied by its producer to another.

The reference in (a) to the purposes for which the product has been marketed may indicate that a balance has to be struck between known risks associated with a product and the benefits which it seeks to confer. With regard to (b), a product which is clearly intended for a particular use may not be defective if it causes damage when put to an entirely different use. With (c) it is the time of supply by the producer to another which is relevant not the time of supply to the consumer.

Liability under the Act is considerably stricter that under common law.

One case that illustrates this is *A and others v National Blood Authority* (2001). The claimants had been infected with Hepatitis C, through blood transfusions which had used blood products obtained from infected donors. The defendants argued that the product was as safe as might be expected, and also that the defect in the particular transfusion could not have been detected). Given the strict liability under the Act, it was held that factors which would have been relevant in a negligence action were completely irrelevant and the defendants were found to be liable under the Consumer Protection Act.

Definition of "damage"

Section 5(1) defines damage for the purposes of Part 1 as death or personal injury, or loss of or damage to property (including land), although claims for damage to property are limited in several respects. First, the defendant will not be liable for damage to the defective product itself, nor for damage to any product supplied with a defective component comprised in it. Secondly, there is no liability unless, at the time of the damage, the property was "of a description of property ordinarily intended for private use, occupation of consumption" and was intended by the claimant mainly for such purposes (s.5(3)). A person who suffers damage to his business property must therefore sue in negligence as opposed to under the Act.

Defences

Section 4(1) of the Act provides for defences as follows:

a) The defect is attributable to compliance either with a domestic enactment or community law.

b) The defendant did not at any time supply the product to another. A broad definition is given to "supply" in a later part of the act to include not only the usual types of supply contract but also gifts.

c) The defendant supplied the product otherwise than in the course of his business and either he does not fall within s.2(2) (he is not a producer, "own brander" or importer) or he does so only by virtue of things done other wise than in a view to profit.

d) The defect did not exist at the relevant time. By s.4(2) the "relevant time" means, in relation to electricity, the time at which it was generated. With all other products it means, in the case of a defendant to whom s.2(2) applies the time when he supplied the product to another and, in the case of a supplier, the time of the last supply by a person who is within the ambit of that section.

e) The state of scientific and technical knowledge at the relevant time was not such that a producer of products of the same description as the product in question might be expected to have discovered the defect if it had existed in his products while they were under his control. This is called the "development risk" or "state of the art" defence

f) The defect constituted a defect in a product containing the defendant's component part (or raw material) and was wholly attributable to the design of the overall product or to compliance by the defendant with instructions given by the producer of the overall product.

Common law negligence

Where the Consumer Protection Act does not apply, the claimant must rely on existing common law remedies. If the claimant acquires defective goods under a sale or similar supply contract the remedy is to sue the supplier for breach of implied undertakings relating to quality. Although these contractual obligations are generally imposed only upon those who supply in the course of business, they are strict and entitle the claimant to recover both in respect of goods which simply fail to work or which are less valuable than those contracted for, and where the defect causes personal injury or damage to property. If the claimant does not have a contract, an action in tort may be pursued.

The duty of the manufacturer

The duty owed by a manufacturer to the consumer was stated in Donoghue v Stevenson (Hl 1932) by Lord Atkins as follows:

"A manufacturer of products, which he sells in such a form as to show that he intends them to reach the ultimate consumer in the form in which they left him with no reasonable possibility of immediate examination, and with the knowledge that the absence of reasonable care in the preparation or putting up of the products will result in an injury to the consumer's life or property, owes a duty to the consumer to take that reasonable care".

The term "products" includes not only comestibles, but many other diverse products such as shoes, vehicles, toys and so on. the manufacturer's duty extend to the packaging of the product and to any labels, warnings or instructions for use which accompany it. If the manufacturer of a finished product incorporates a component made by another, he is under a duty to check on its suitability and may be liable for failure to do so should it turn out to be defective. Where products are already in circulation when the defect is discovered the manufacturer must take reasonable steps to warn of the danger or to recall the products.

Manufacturer and ultimate consumer

The term "manufacturer" has been interpreted to include any person who actively does something to the goods to create the danger, such as assemblers, servicers, repairers, installers and erectors.

In *Malfroot v Noxal Limited* (HC 1935) an assembler was held liable when the side car which he had negligently fitted to a motor cycle came adrift and injured the plaintiff. Mere suppliers may come within the rule, even though they may be unaware of the danger and do nothing to create it. In the case *Andrews v Hopkinson* (HC 1957) a second hand car dealer was liable for failing to check that an 18 year-old car was roadworthy, with the result that the plaintiff was injured in a collision caused by a failure of the steering.

Apart from the end user of the product, the "ultimate consumer" is any person who may foreseeably be affected by it. In the case *Stennet v Hancock and Peters* (HC 1939) the defendant was held liable for negligently fitting a metal flange to a wheel of a lorry, so that it came off when the vehicle was in motion and struck the plaintiff.

Proof of negligence and damage

The burden rests upon the claimant as in any other negligence action. However, damage caused by a defect in manufacture as opposed to a defect in design, may easily give rise to an inference of negligence. On the other hand, if it is equally probable that the defect arose after the manufacturing process and is wholly unconnected with anything that the manufacturer may have done, claimant will fail.

The defendant will no longer escape liability however, merely by showing that he had a fool-proof system of manufacture and quality control, because the very fact of the defect may be evidence of negligence in the operation of that system by a person for whom the defendant is vicariously liable. Where the alleged defect is in relation to the design of the product, the claimant may face greater difficulty in that the issue of negligence is to be judged in the light of current knowledge which must be proved to have been such as to render the damage foreseeable.

As far as damage is concerned, liability only exists in respect of personal injury or damage to other property, although consequential financial loss is also recoverable. Pure economic loss is, however, irrecoverable.

****

Ch. 3

BUSINESS LAW-EMPLOYMENT LAW-EMPLOYMENT CONTRACTS

Into every contract of employment are implied a number of obligations in so far as these are not inconsistent with the express terms of the individual contract of employment. These duties are based on principles developed by the courts in the decided cases.

Implied duties may be classified as follows:
a) to be ready and willing to work;

b) to use reasonable care and skill;

c) to obey lawful orders;

d) to take care of the employers property;

e) to act in good faith.

To be ready and willing to work
The fundamental duty owed to an employer by an employee is to be turn up to work and to work at the direction of the employer in return for wages. Two interesting cases have arisen in relation to this. In Miles v Wakefield Metropolitan District Council (1987) M was a superintendent registrar of births deaths and marriages, working 37 hours per week, three of which were on Saturday morning. As part of industrial action, M refused to carry out marriages on Saturday mornings, although he was willing to do his other work. Wages were deducted, M sued for lost wages and the employer won,

with the House of Lords (Supreme Court) saying that where an employee refuses to perform the full range of duties and had been told that he would not be paid if he did not, then the employers were entitled to withhold the whole of his remuneration, (3hrs) although he attended for work and carried out a substantial part of his duties.

To use reasonable care and skill

This has two aspects:

a) The duty not to be unduly negligent.

b) The duty to be reasonably competent.

If an employee is negligent during the course of his work, he may be regarded as being in breach of contract. In Lister v Romford Ice and Cold Storage Ltd (1957) a lorry driver, employed by the company, carelessly reversed his lorry and injured a fellow employee, who was his father. The employers paid damages to the father but claimed indemnity from the son, because of negligence. This was held to be the case.

Duty to be reasonably competent

If an employee is incompetent this may be a breach of contract. In Hamer v Cornelius (1858) this was held to be the case.

To obey lawful orders

An employee is under a duty to obey all the lawful orders of his employer, i.e. those which are within the scope of the contract. In Price v Mouat (1862) a lace salesman was ordered to card (pack) lace but he refused and was dismissed without notice. He claimed wrongful dismissal and this was held because the order was not one which was within the scope of his contract. An employee, therefore, is not obliged to do any act, which is deemed to fall outside the ambit of his individual contract of employment. The question of the introduction of new technology has caused problems here and must be linked to the scope of managerial prerogative in introducing new work techniques. In Cresswell v Board of Inland Revenue (1984) the Revenue wished to introduce a computer system to assist with the PAYE system. The majority of the work associated with the system had been done manually. Did the employers have the ability to change the nature of the working system? Did the employers have the ability to change the nature of the working system? Held: employees were expected to adopt the new methods and techniques in performing their contracts if the employer provided the necessary training in new skills.

To take care of employers property

An employer is under an obligation to take reasonable care of his employer's property. In Superflux v Plaisted (1958) the defendant had been in charge of a team of vacuum cleaner salesmen and had negligently allowed fourteen cleaners to be stolen from his van. Held: he was in breach of his contract of employment.

To act in good faith

His implied duty has several different aspects, which together form the basis of a relationship of trust. There is the duty not to make a secret profit, i.e. not to accept bribes.

This principal was clear from the case of Reading v AG (1951) which concerned a member of the armed forces, in which Lord Normand said:--- though the relation of a member of his majesty's forces is not accurately described as that of a servant under a contract of service--he owes to the Crown a duty as full fiduciary as the duty of a servant to his master--and in consequence--all profits and advantages gained by the use of his military status are to be for the benefit of the Crown'.

Duty to disclose certain information.

There appears to be no general duty on an employee to inform his employer of his misconduct and deficiencies: Bell v Lever Brothers (1932). However, there is one important exception, namely where the employment of that particular person is made more hazardous by virtue of an undisclosed defect on part of the employee.

121

Covenants in restraint of trade

A covenant in restraint of trade is a clause in a contract, which purports to limit an employees rights to seek employment when and where he chooses upon leaving his employment. This is usually done as a protective measure by an employer when he might suffer as a result of disclosure of confidential information or for other such reasons.

There are difficulties however, in enforcing such covenants and the employer has to demonstrate that the covenant is justified. A court will look at such factors as the time that the covenant runs, geographical area that it covers and public interest when considering the reasonableness of such covenants.

If a covenant is found to be unreasonable, the contract as a whole is not necessarily regarded as void, unless it is impossible to distinguish the covenant from the rest of the contract. If the covenant can be severed from the rest of the contract, without altering the nature of the agreement, the unreasonable clause may be struck out: see Commercial Plastics LTD v Vincent (1965).

If an employer breaks the contract of employment by wrongfully dismissing an employee, the employee may disregard any covenant in the contract which purports to limit his right to seek employment elsewhere: see General Billposting v Atkinson (1909).

Patents

At common law, unless the contract dealt with the matter, an employee would not normally be entitled to the benefit of any invention made by him if to allow him to do so would be a contravention of the implied duty of the employee to act in good faith.

The Patents Act 1977, ss-39-47, gives ownership of an invention to the employee inventor unless the invention was made in the course of the duties for which he was employed. Any disputes are dealt with by the patents court.

Duties of the employer

By virtue of common law, and a number of statutory provisions, employers have a considerable number of obligations towards employees. The main examples are:

To pay contractually agreed remuneration

An employer is under no obligation to provide work as long as remuneration is paid. This however, has been questioned in recent times, particularly in relation to skilled employees. Lord Denning said, in Langston v AUEW (1973): 'In these days an employer, when employing a skilled man, is bound to provide him with work. By which I mean that the man should be given the opportunity of doing his work when it is available and when he is ready and willing to do it'. Therefore, a failure to provide work of a nature that the employee is used to could be regarded as constructive dismissal.

There are three exceptions to the rule, one is piecework, the second is where the nature of the employment is such that the actual performance of the work forms part of the consideration supplied by the employer, the employee may be entitled to compensation over and above the contractual wages. These situations are sometimes referred to as 'names in lights' clauses. the other exception is when an employee is taking part in limited industrial action.

National Minimum Wage

From April 1999 the amount of pay an employee is entitled to receive is governed by the National Minimum Wage Act (NMW) 1998.

The Act by s.1 covers worker's which is wider than the traditional definition of employee in employment law. Essentially, the NMW will apply to a workers gross pay, which will include incentive payments. Certain other benefits will be excluded from the calculation, such as tips.

From October 2013 the main adult rate for workers aged 21 and over is be £6.31 per hour. The rate for worker 18-20 is £5.03 per hour. For workers under 18 the rate is £3.72 Apprentices £2.68 per hour..

The above figures are correct at the time of writing. For up to date figures and other information concerning the NMW contact ACAS through their website or the Pay and Work Rights Helpline on 0800 917 2368.

The following groups are not entitled to the National Minimum Wage:

- self-employed people
- company directors
- volunteers or voluntary workers

123

- workers on a government employment programme, eg the Work Programme
- family members of the employer living in the employer's home
- non-family members living in the employer's home who share in the work and leisure activities, are treated as one of the family and aren't charged for meals or accommodation (eg au pairs)
- workers younger than school leaving age (usually 16)
- higher and further education students on a work placement up to 1 year
- workers on government pre-apprenticeships schemes
- people on certain European Union programmes
- people working in a Jobcentre Plus Work trial for 6 weeks
- members of the armed forces
- share fishermen
- prisoners
- people living and working in a religious community

Work experience and internships

A person won't get minimum wage if they are:

- a student doing work experience as part of a higher education course
- of compulsory school age (usually 16)
- a volunteer or doing voluntary work
- on a government or European programme
- work shadowing

Voluntary work

A person is classed as doing voluntary work if they can only get certain limited benefits (eg reasonable travel or lunch expenses) and they are working for a:

- charity
- voluntary organisation or associated fund-raising body
- statutory body

Pay reference period

The NMW is set at an hourly rate but that does not mean a person must be paid at least the NMW for each hour they work. Rather, their average hourly pay must be at least the NMW as worked out over the 'pay reference period'. The pay reference period is the interval between which they are normally paid. If they are normally paid on a daily basis their pay reference period is one day, if they are paid weekly it will be one week and if monthly, one month.

The pay reference period cannot be longer than one month. If they are normally paid quarterly, they have a right to be paid at least the NMW on average during each month within that quarter. Most people can easily work out whether they are getting the NMW by dividing their pay (before tax and other permitted deductions by the number of hours worked.

Permitted deductions

An employer is legally required to make the following deductions from an employees pay:

- Income tax
- National Insurance
- Student loan payments
- Pension contributions
- Trade union subscriptions

There are certain payments and deductions that do not count towards NMW pay. These include deductions and payments made by an employer for:

-Tools, uniforms etc. which the employer provides for the employee to do their job
-Expenses paid for costs incurred in your job
-Goods and services connected to employment which the employer retains for their own use and benefit, such as the use of transport to and from work.

It is unlawful for employers to make such deductions or require a person to make such payments if it means that they do not receive the NMW.

From 2009 onwards it is unlawful for employers to count tips or gratuities received from customers towards NMW pay. In addition, any premiums of pay which are received on top of basic rate for working at special times are not counted along with any other special allowances.

Benefits in kind also cannot count towards the NMW. The only exception is a set amount for accommodation. Examples of benefits in kind can be meals, staff car, medical insurance, gym membership, lunch vouchers, childcare vouchers, eye test vouchers and employers contributions towards a pension.

To treat employees with trust and confidence

In Courtaulds Northern Textiles Ltd v Andrew (1978) the EAT held'---there is an implied term in a contract of employment that employers will not, without reasonable and proper cause, conduct themselves in a manner calculated or likely to destroy or seriously damage the relationship of trust or confidence between the parties' A series of cases have firmly established this principle.

To observe provisions relating to holidays

The written statement provided to employees under the 1996 Act ought to state the holidays to which the employee is entitled and whether the employee is entitled to holiday pay and if so how much. There are relatively few statutory provisions. Section 94 of the Factories Act 1961 provides that women and young persons who work in factories must have a holiday on bank holidays and the Wages Councils and Agricultural Wages Board have the power to fix holiday pay for workers in the industries over which they have jurisdiction.

To observe provisions relating to hours of work

The hours which an employee is required to work are determined by reference to his individual contract of employment and the written statement supplied to the employee ought to state these. There are certain statutory provisions, section 7 of the Sex Discrimination Act 1986 (now replaced by the Equality Act 2010) removed the majority of limitations imposed concerning the hours to be worked by women. Part V1 of the Factories Act 1961 limits the working day to no more than nine hours for young people.

In addition, see below, the Working Time Regulations 1998. These have introduced specific regulations controlling the working week and covers a broad variety of workers not only employees.

To permit employees time off work for public duties
The 1996 Act provides that an employer must permit an employee to have time off work for the purpose of carrying out work as:

a) Justice of the peace (work relating to this)
b) a member of a local authority
c) a member of a statutory tribunal
d) a member of a regional health authority or an Area or District educational establishment.
e) a member of a governing body of a local authority maintained educational establishment.

A number of categories of employees are excluded from this right, under the 1996 Act. Under the 1996 Act a pregnant employee has the right not to be unreasonably refused time off work with pay in order that she may keep appointments for receiving anti-natal care. Evidence of pregnancy and appointment must be produced if requested by employer.

To indemnify employees
An employer is under an obligation to indemnify his employees in respect of any expenses incurred in performing their duties under the contract of employment, for example traveling expenses. In certain circumstances however, the employee may be under an obligation to indemnify the employer for any loss sustained: see Lister v Romford Ice and Cold Storage LTD (1957)

To provide references
There is no obligation on an employer to supply character references for

127

employees although, in practice, employers normally supply them since failure to provide one speaks for itself. The legal effect of references means that if an employer does provide one, it ought to be correct for several reasons: If a reference is defamatory, the defamed employee may bring an action against the employer, although the defence of qualified privilege is available to the employer, i.e. the employer may show that the statements were made without malice.

Negligent misstatement. A person who acts in reliance on a reference, which has been issued negligently, may apparently bring an action to recover any loss sustained as a consequence.

Working Time Rights
Under Europe's Working Time Directive, most people now have seven basic rights to proper time off, rest breaks and paid holiday.

Who has working time rights?
These working time rights apply to all employees and workers from the first day of employment. The rights apply to most agency workers, homeworkers and freelancers. Only those who are self-employed and are genuinely running their own business do not have the right to paid annual leave.

Working time rights do not apply to:
- individuals who are self-employed and who are genuinely running their own business
- individuals who can choose freely their hours and duration of work (such as a managing executive)
- the armed forces, emergency services and police are excluded in some circumstances
- domestic servants in private houses

Working time rules also apply differently to some groups of workers (e.g. those who have to travel a long distance from home to get to work) and in some sectors or workplaces (e.g. security, hospitals, or air, road or sea transport) or when there is an emergency or accident.

Rest breaks

An employee has the right to a rest break of at least 20 minutes where they work for a continuous period of six hours or more during a working day / shift. If under 18 however, they are entitled to a 30-minute break after working four and a half hours.

Additional or longer breaks may be provided for in the contract. A lunch break or coffee break can count as a rest break.

The requirements are:

* the break must be in one block
* it cannot be taken off one end of the working day - it must be somewhere in the middle
* An employee is allowed to spend it away from the workplace

An employer can say when rest breaks can be taken provided they meet these requirements.

An employee does not have an automatic right to be paid for rest breaks. Whether they receive pay for rest breaks will depend on their contract.

Daily rest periods

An employee has the right to a rest period of 11 uninterrupted hours every working day.

If they are under 18, they are entitled to a 12 hour uninterrupted rest period per working day. This rest period must be continuous and uninterrupted.

Weekly rest breaks

An employee has the right to a rest period of either:

- 24 hours in every 7 day period or
- 48 hours in every fortnight

This rest period must be continuous and uninterrupted. Employers have a duty to make sure that an employee takes their breaks.

48 hour working time limit

An employee has the right not to work more than 48 hours a week on average. This limit is averaged over a 17-week period. This means that it is legal to work more than 48 hours in some weeks, so long as they work less in others.

An employee can opt out of this right unless they work at night, but should not be pressured to opt out. The opt-out must be voluntary and must be in writing.

An employee has a right to opt back in again to working time protection at anytime, but they must give the employer at least 7 days notice. They may be required to give more notice - up to 3 months, if they previously agreed to this with their employer in writing.

Young workers and working time limits

The weekly working time limits for young workers are 8 hours a day and 40 hours per week.

For the majority of young workers these are absolute limits. A young worker's working time is not averaged over a reference period, so in one week they must not work more than 40 hours. The opt-out provisions do not apply to young workers. Please see the section below.

Young workers will only be able to work more than 8 hours per day, or 40 hours per week if they are needed to:

- keep the continuity of service or production
- respond to a surge in demand for a service or product

And provided that:

- there is no adult available to do the work
- their training needs are not negatively affected

What counts as working time?

As well as time spent doing their job, an employee's working time will include time spent on:

- job related training
- job related travelling time, although not time spent travelling
- overtime, whether paid or unpaid
- time spent 'on-call' at the workplace
- working lunches
- time spent working abroad if working for a UK- based company

What does not count as working time?

Working time does not include:
- breaks when no work is done, e.g. lunch breaks
- time when on-call away from the workplace (although time spent working when away from the workplace, e.g. answering calls at home, will count as working time)
- paid or unpaid holidays

Working in more than one job

If an employee works for more than one employer, the combined time that they work should not exceed more than 48 hours, unless they have signed the opt out with their employers.

Night work

Regular night workers should not work more than eight hours in each 24-hour period. The Working Time Regulations allow for night work to be averaged over a 17-week period in the same way as weekly hours of work. There is no opt out from the night work limits.

If an employee's night work involves special hazards or heavy physical or mental strain, they cannot be made to work more than eight hours in any 24 hour period.

Young workers under 18 are not permitted to work between 10pm-6am.

Before night work can commence an employer must have offered the employee an opportunity to undertake a free health assessment unless they have previously had a health assessment which is still valid.

The employer must then offer free health assessments at regular intervals, to ensure it is still safe for the employee to undertake night work.

Where an employer is advised by a doctor/registered medical practitioner that the employee cannot undertake night work, the employer should where possible, transfer them to work which they are suited and is work within normal working time (day time).

It is good practice for an employer to provide the employee with enhanced pay rates for doing night work or unsocial hours. But the employee will not have a right to receive enhanced pay for doing night work, unless their contract provides for it.

If an employer does not permit an employee to take rest breaks or daily or weekly breaks, they can make a complaint to an Employment Tribunal.

If an employer pressurises an employee to work more than 48 hours when they have not signed an opt-out or does not comply with night work rules, the employee can make a complaint through the Pay and Work Rights helpline.

Holiday pay

If a person works regular hours and get the same pay each week, then holiday pay is simply the same as their normal pay. If the normal pay includes regular bonuses, shift premiums or contractual overtime payments, then these should also be included in holiday pay.

If weekly pay varies because hours vary from week to week, then weekly holiday pay should be the average weekly pay earned over the last 12 weeks.

Maternity and parental pay and leave

Apart from important protection from unfair dismissal because of pregnancy, the Employment Rights Act 1996 provided four further protections in relation to pregnancy - the right to maternity leave, the right to return to work after maternity leave, the right to time off for ante-natal care and the right to maternity pay. The section of the above Act dealing with maternity leave was replaced in its entirety by the Employment Relations Act 1999 Part 1, Schedule 4 which in turn has been amended by the 2002 Employment Act, the provisions of which came into force on April 6th 2003. An amendment was also made by the Maternity and Parental Leave Regulations 2008.

In addition to the above, pregnancy and maternity is now one of the protected characteristics in the Equality Act 2010 and there is now implied into every woman's term of employment a maternity equality clause (s 73 Equality Act 2010). The act protects women from direct discrimination (s 13(1)) and indirect discrimination (s 19(1)) in relation to pregnancy and maternity.

Right to maternity leave

Part V111 of the 1996 Employment Rights Act contains provisions for maternity rights that are further detailed in the Maternity and Parental Leave Regulations 1999. The Directive gives all pregnant employees a general right to maternity leave.

Under the 1999 Employment Rights Act, which came into force on the 15th December 1999, the periods of leave were renamed. Maternity leave became ordinary maternity leave (OML) and additional absence became additional maternity leave (AML).

The regulations now clarify that the term remuneration is now limited to 'sums payable by way of wages or salary'. This means, for example, that women will automatically be entitled to retain a company car and a mobile phone and to receive a performance bonus which is not salary.

All pregnant employees are entitled to 52 weeks maternity leave. This consists of 26 weeks Ordinary Maternity Leave and 26 weeks Additional Maternity Leave. This is available to all employees from the first day of employment. The employee can choose when they start their leave but the earliest it can start is 11 weeks before the baby is due.

The only women not entitled to maternity leave are:

- Share fisherwomen
- Women who normally work abroad (unless they have a work connection with the UK
- Policewomen and women serving in the armed forces

Compulsory maternity leave

An employer may not permit an employee to work during her compulsory maternity period. Compulsory maternity leave is a period of two weeks commencing on the day on which childbirth occurs. An employer who allows a pregnant person to work can be fined.

Giving notice to the employer

In order to qualify for maternity leave the employer must be informed by the end of the 15th week before the baby is due:

- that the employee is pregnant
- the week in which the baby is expected; and
- the date when the employee intends to start ordinary maternity leave.

There is no obligation to put this in writing unless asked to. However, it is a good idea to do so. Once the employer has been informed that maternity leave will be taken they have 28 days to inform you when maternity leave starts.

If the employee has already a contractual right to maternity pay/leave, she may exercise her right to the more favourable terms. If there is a redundancy situation during the leave period and it is not practicable because of the redundancy for the employer to continue to employ her under her existing contract, she is entitled to be offered a suitable vacancy before her employment ends. If a woman intends to return to work before the end of maternity leave, 56 days notice must be given. Since women who qualify now have the right to take Additional Maternity Leave, and there is no obligation to notify the employer during the initial notification, then until notification of a return to work is given, the women will retain the right to return but not pay.

Work during the maternity leave period

Regulation 12A provides that an employee may carry out up to ten days work for her employer during her statutory maternity period (excluding the compulsory maternity period) without bringing her maternity period to an end.

Time off for Ante-natal care

To qualify for this right the employee must have made an appointment for ante-natal care on the advice of a doctor, midwife or health visitor. The employer may not refuse time off for the first visit, but for further appointments, the employer may ask for a certificate or appointment card or other evidence.

Statutory Maternity Pay

The Social Security Act of 1996 and the Statutory Maternity Pay regulations of the same year entitle certain employees to statutory maternity pay. This has been amended by the 2002 Employment Act. SMP is paid for a maximum of 39 weeks. For the first six weeks of maternity leave SMP is paid at 90% of the average gross weekly earnings (before tax and NI) for the remaining 33 weeks it is paid at 90% of gross weekly earnings or £136.78 a week, whichever is the lower.

To claim SMP, a person must tell their employer, 28 days before maternity leave, that they are pregnant and will be off work because of birth. A medical certificate has to be provided.

When is SMP paid?

How long SMP is paid for depends on when the baby is due. It is paid up to

39 weeks. The earliest a person can start maternity leave and start to get SMP is 11 weeks before the baby is due. The latest date to start maternity leave and receiving SMP is the week after the week when the baby is born.

If a person is sick with a pregnancy related illness before the baby is due, SMP will start the week following the week that sickness began. If a person is sick with a non-pregnancy related illness they can claim Statutory Sick pay until the week that the baby is due.

Maternity Allowance

If an employee is not entitled to get SMP they may be entitled to maternity allowance instead.

This is administered through jobcentre plus and a person might get maternity benefit if:

- they are employed, but not eligible for SMP
- they are registered self-employed and paying class C National Insurance Contributions (NIC's) or hold a Small Earnings Exemption Certificate
- they have been very recently employed or self-employed.

Further, they may be eligible if:

- they have been employed or self employed for at least 26 weeks in the 'test period' (66 weeks up to and including the week before the week the baby is due) part weeks count as full weeks; and
- they earned £30 a week averaged over any 13 week period in the test period.

Returning to work after maternity leave

There is an automatic right to return to work after maternity leave and it is assumed the person will do so unless they state otherwise. If a person decides to return earlier than the date notified by the employer, then at least 56 days notice must be given of returning.

Parental leave

The Maternity and Parental Leave Regulations 1999 provide that every person who cares for a young child, or has recently adopted a child, can take time off from work at his or her own convenience to care for that child. Minimum provisions are set for leave, preconditions are set for leave and the notice that an employee has to give an employer before leave can be taken is set out. Employers and employees can agree to vary these provisions by using a workforce agreement as long as it is equal to or more favorable than the statutory provisions.

Any employee who has one year's continuous employment at the date the leave is due to start, and who has, or expects to have, responsibility for a child at that time can apply to take parental leave. A person will have responsibility for a child under the regulations if he/she has parental responsibility under the Children Act 1989 or is registered as the father under the provision of the Births and Deaths Register Act.

The leave entitlement is up to 4 weeks unpaid parental leave per year while the child is under the age of 5, subject to an overall maximum of 13 weeks leave in respect of each child. If there are twins, each parent can take 26 weeks parental leave. The leave for the parent of a disabled child is 18 weeks per child.

Employers can request records of leave already taken with previous employers; the entitlement is per child and not per employer.

The employee can take leave in blocks of 1 week (or blocks of one day where the child is disabled) to a maximum of 4 weeks in respect of an individual child in an individual year.

(Part time employees get a pro-rata entitlement.)

Paternity leave

In addition, the 2002 Employment Act widened the scope and range of paternity leave. The Act introduced the right to two weeks paid leave in addition to the 13 weeks unpaid leave. This became effective from April 2003. Leave must be taken within 8 weeks of the birth of the child or placement of the child through adoption.

For employees to claim paternity leave they must:

- Be employed and have worked for their employer for at least 26 weeks before the end of the 15th week before the expected week of childbirth; and

• Be the biological father of the child, or be married to or be the partner of the baby's mother (this includes same sex partners, whether or not they are registered civil partners); and

• Have some responsibility for the child's upbringing; and

• Have given the employer the correct notice to take paternity leave.

• Paternity leave can be taken as a single block of either one or two weeks.

All terms and conditions of employment remain intact during the period of paternity leave except the right to remuneration. Employees are entitled to return to the jobs they had before they took paternity leave.

The Additional Paternity Leave Regulations 2010

The Additional Paternity Leave Regulations 2010 recognise that mothers can often be the main earner for the family and aims to promote shared parenting. The regulations enable eligible employees to have the right to take additional paternity leave and pay. However the right only affects parents of children that are due to be born on or after the 3rd April 2011 or where one or both of the parents have received adoptive notification on or after the 3rd April 2011 that they have been matched with a child for adoption.

Additional Paternity Leave (APL) will allow a father to take up to 26 weeks leave to care for a child and also allows mothers to 'transfer' up to 6 months of maternity leave to their partner. APL will only be able to start 20 weeks after the birth of the child and must end no later then the child's first birthday. In the case of adoption, the earliest APL can start is 20 weeks after the child was placed for adoption and must end no later than one year after the placement began. There is no requirement for the father's leave to begin directly after the mother has returned from statutory maternity Leave or statutory adoption leave and have/or ended their entitlement to statutory maternity or adoption pay, or maternity allowance. In addition, in order to be eligible for Additional Paternity Leave and Pay (APLP), a father must be continuously employed by the same employer for at least 26 weeks, ending with the relevant week and also remain in the same employment until he starts his leave. In the case of a birth, the relevant week is 15 weeks before the baby is due and in the case of adoption it is the week the adopter is matched with a child for adoption.

Fathers seeking to take APLP must provide a declaration to their employers at least 8 weeks before they wish to start their leave, confirmation of when they intend the leave to start and finish, a declaration stating that they wish to take the leave to care for a child and that the eligibility requirements have been satisfied. Fathers must also provide a declaration from the mother that provides her employers with her name, address, National Insurance Number and the date she intends to return from maternity leave. The mother must also consent to her employers processing the information and she must confirm that the father has the status he has detailed on his declaration and confirm that he is the only person seeking the leave in respect of the child.

Adoption leave and pay

The 2002 Employment Act creates a right for parents to take adoption leave when permanently adopting a child. An adoptive parent is entitled to take 26 weeks paid adoption leave (known as 'ordinary adoption leave') and up to 26 weeks unpaid adoption leave During ordinary adoption leave, employees will be entitled to receive Statutory Adoption Pay (SAP) for 39 weeks of £136.78 per week (2013-2014) or 90% of earnings, whichever is the lower. You should check with the DTI or DSS for current rates.

Qualifying requirements

To be entitled to take adoption leave, employees must have attained 26 weeks service with their employer at the date the adoption takes place. Leave can be taken at any time after the adoption placement begins. Employees will be required to provide evidence of the adoption to the employer. Only one partner in a couple will be able to take adoption leave. The other partner, male or female, will be able to take paternity leave for 2 weeks and receive SPP. There are statutory notice provisions covering how and when employees must inform employers that they wish to take adoption leave. These are flexible and can be verified with the employer. During the period of ordinary adoption leave the employee is entitled to all their terms and conditions, except the right to remuneration. During the period of additional adoption leave, the employee is in the same position as someone on additional maternity leave – namely that whilst most of the terms and conditions of employment will be suspended, those relating to notice, confidentiality, implied terms of mutual trust and confidence, redundancy terms and disciplinary and grievance procedures will remain in place. The right to return after either ordinary or additional adoption leave mirror's the provisions for ordinary and additional maternity leave respectively.

Statutory right to request a contractual variation-flexible working

The 2002 Employment Act introduced a right to request a contractual variation, where the reason for the request relates to a young child. The 2006 Work and Families Act extended the right, from April 2007 to an employee who cares for, or who expects to care for, an adult. A carer is defined as an employee who is, or expects to be, caring for an adult who is married to, or is the partner or civil partner of the employee or who is a near relative of the employee or falls into neither of these categories but lives at the same address as the employer.

Applications can only be made by parents or potential carers who have worked continuously for an employer for 26 weeks before applying and whose children are under 17 at the time of the application or by parents of disabled children under the age of 18. An employee can request changes to his or her terms and conditions and, in particular, the following:

- Hours of work
- The times when the employee is required to work.
- Where the employee is required to work
- Such other aspects of his or her terms and conditions of employment as the Secretary of State may specify

Procedure for flexible working request

A request for flexible working must:

- State that it is a request for flexible working'
- Specify the changes applied for and the date on which they are to become effective and:
- Explain what effect the changes have on the workplace and how they can propose they can be dealt with

Only one request can be made per year.

Employer's response

The employer must consider the application and can only refuse the application on certain given grounds. These are as follows:

- The burden of additional costs
- The detrimental effect on ability to meet customer demand
- The inability to reorganize work amongst existing staff
- The detrimental impact on quality
- The detrimental impact on performance
- The insufficiency of work during the period the employee proposes to work: and
- Any planned structural changes

Regulations will provide a timetable detailing how the employer must respond to a request for flexible working.

It is likely that an employer will be required to arrange a meeting to consider the request within 28 days of receipt. The employer must give a decision within 14 days of the meeting. If the employee's request is refused, the employer must give grounds for the decision.

An employee will be entitled to appeal but must set out their grounds for appeal. The employer must hear the appeal within 14 days and a decision must be given to the employee within 14 days of the appeal hearing.

Remedies

Where a request has been refused an employee can bring a claim at the Employment Tribunal but only where the employer:

- Has failed to comply with the statutory procedure in considering the application.
- Has refused the request on a ground that is different to the specified grounds above: or
- Has made the decision based on incorrect facts
- Therefore, there is no jurisdiction for the Employment Tribunal to hear a claim if the employee is merely unhappy about the decision.

If the Tribunal finds against the employer it can:

- Order reconsideration of the issue and/or
- Make an award for compensation

In addition, there will also be the right for employees not to be subjected to a detriment, including dismissal by the employer if they have made an application for flexible working, they have appealed against a refusal to allow flexible working, they have brought proceedings in the Employment Tribunal in respect of a refusal to allow flexible working, or the employee has alleged circumstances which could constitute a ground for bringing such proceedings.

Part Time Workers

There have been significant advances relating to the position of part time workers in relation to remuneration and terms and conditions of employment. The Part-Time Workers (Prevention of Less Favourable Treatment) Regulations 2000 introduced new rights for part time workers. The Part-Time Workers Regulations ensure that Britain's Part Timers are not treated less favourably than comparable full-timers in their terms and conditions, unless it is objectively justified. This means part-timers are entitled to a range of benefits, including:

- The same hourly rates of pay
- The same access to company pension schemes
- The same entitlements to annual leave and maternity/parental leave

on a pro-rata basis
- The same entitlement to contractual sick pay
- No less favourable treatment in access to training

Two amendments in 2002 introduced Comparators and occupational pension schemes (regulation 2).

Under the original regulations, part-timers had to compare themselves to full-timers employed under the same type of contract. This meant that, for example a part-timer on a fixed-term contract should compare themselves to a full-timer on a fixed-term contract. This is no longer the case

The other amendment is that of access to occupational pension schemes. Under Regulation 8 (8) of the Part-Time Workers Regulations, where an Employment Tribunal has upheld a complaint from a part-timer for equal access to an occupational pension scheme, the remedies which the tribunal orders may go back no further than two years. In 2001, the House of Lords (Supreme Court) held that this was unlawful in that it contravened European law on the equal treatment of men and women, and could no longer be maintained. As a consequence the law has now been amended to remove the two-year time limit.

****

3.2

TERMINATING EMPLOYMENT

There are a number of ways in which a contract of employment may come to an end-termination by way of contract, termination in breach of contract and termination by methods external to the contract.

At common law, a contract of employment can be validly terminated by an employer giving notice to an employee in accordance with the terms of the contract or, in the absence of such a term, by giving reasonable notice. If sufficient notice was given, the employee had no further rights and this meant that dismissal could be entirely arbitrary. However, in recent times provisions have been introduced whereby an employee may be entitled to compensation for loss of job despite the fact that he was given notice.

It should be noted that once notice has been given, it can only effectively be withdrawn with the consent of the other party.

Dismissal with notice

The length of notice, which must be given by an employer to an employee, is determined by reference to the following criteria to be applied in the following order:

a) Express terms of the contract. If the contract of employment expressly provides for a period of notice, this must be observed unless that period is less than the statutory minimum to which that particular employee is entitled under d) below.

b) In the absence of an express term it may be impossible to imply a term into the contract, for example, by custom. Again, such a period may not be less than the statutory custom.

c) If there is no express or implied term of the contract, the courts may rely on a reasonable period. What is "reasonable" depends upon such factors as the status of the employee, salary, length of employment with that employer, age etc. The "reasonable" period cannot be less than the statutory minimum.

d) Statutory minimum. In the absence of any of the above criteria, or where they produce a period less than the following, the statutory minimum in s 86 of the 1996 Act (ERA) must be applied in respect of those employees covered by that section. Section 86 provides that for an employee continuously employed for between one month and two years, the notice period is one week; for an employee employed for more than two years, he is entitled to one week for each year of continuous employment subject to a maximum of twelve weeks notice after twelve years of employment. These rights do not apply to a contract for the performance of a specific task, which is not expected to last for more than three months.

Constructive dismissal

Constructive dismissal is when an employee forced to leave their job against their will because of their employer's conduct.

The reasons an employee leaves their job must be serious, for example, an employer:

- don't pay an employee or suddenly demotes them for no reason

- forces the employee to accept unreasonable changes to how they work - e.g. tells them to work night shifts when their contract is only for day work

- let other employees harass or bully them

The employer's breach of contract may be one serious incident or a series of incidents that are serious when taken together.

Summary dismissal

Summary dismissal is where an employer dismisses an employee without giving the employee the amount of notice to which that individual is entitled. If there is no justification, such dismissal is wrongful and an action can be

146

brought. The remedy for wrongful dismissal is damages representing the loss of wages during the period of notice that ought to have been given. In addition, wrongful dismissal may also be unfair dismissal within the meaning of the 1978 Act.

Circumstances which justify summary dismissal

The question of what justifies summary dismissal is not one that can be answered with a simple rule since each case must be decided according to the particular circumstances. However, a general principle has emerged that summary dismissal is justified if the conduct of the employee is such that it prevents further satisfactory continuance of the relationship. This was the finding in Sinclair v Neighbour (1967).

The status of the employee in question is a relevant consideration as is the fact that the employee has a history of misconduct as opposed to an isolated incident.

Dismissals Procedure

If the contract states that dismissal is to be according to an established pattern (e.g. that there will be two warnings before dismissal occurs) it is a breach of contract if the procedure is not observed. (Tomlinson v L.M.S Rly (1944). If the contract states that the dismissal may only occur for certain specified reasons, a dismissal is wrongful if the reason for the dismissal is other than specified in the contract.

However, it should be noted that the 2002 Employment Act has introduced the obligation on an employer to include a statutory disciplinary and grievance procedure which must be in the contract or written terms and must be followed before any dismissal proceedings can take place.

Waiver of rights

If an employee's conduct justified a summary dismissal, the right must have been exercised within a reasonable time of the conduct, which allegedly justified the action since delay may amount to a waiver of the breach of contract.

Employee leaving

An employee is entitled to terminate employment at any time by giving the amount of notice required by the contract. If the employee is deemed to have been entitled to terminate employment by reason of the employer's conduct that may constitute a constructive dismissal and the fact that he gave notice makes no difference.

If an employer's attitude causes an employee to terminate his contract without notice, this may well constitute constructive dismissal and the employee may act accordingly.

Termination by agreement

The parties to a contract of employment as with any other contract, may terminate their relationship by agreement at any time upon such terms as they may agree, e.g. payment of money as a golden handshake. It should be noted that a termination by agreement is not a dismissal for the purposes of the redundancy and unfair dismissals provisions of the 1996 Act. However, the tribunals are concerned to ensure that any alleged agreement to terminate a contract of employment is real and not merely a result of pressure imposed on an employee who is unaware of the significance of agreeing to terminate the contract and who faces dismissal as an alternative to so agreeing.

Termination by frustration

Frustration occurs whenever the law recognises that without default of either party a contractual obligation has become incapable of being performed because the circumstance in which performance would be called for would render it a thing different from that which was undertaken by the contract (Lord Radcliffe in Davis Contractors v Fareham UDC (1956)).

In the context of a contract of employment, the term frustration means that circumstances have arisen, without the fault of either party, that make it impossible for the contract to be performed in the way that may be reasonably expected and the contract automatically terminates without the need for notice to be given. Frustration of the contract is not deemed to be dismissal for legislative purposes. Examples of frustration may be sickness. In Notcutt v

Universal Equipment Co (1986), a worker with 27 years service, who was two years from retirement suffered a permanently incapacitating heart attack. The court decided that this rendered performance of the contract impossible and therefore the contract was frustrated as he was unable to perform his obligation to work. The employee was therefore not entitled to sick pay during his period of notice.

Imprisonment is another example, however this has caused problems. In 1986, the Court of Appeal allowed a four year apprenticeship contract to be frustrated by a six months Borstal sentence: FC Shepherd LTD v Jerrom (1986). In this case court held that such a period of imprisonment made the performance of the contract impossible. As with the sickness, the courts will tend to look at each case on its own merits without applying hard and fast rules.

Action for wrongful dismissal

An employee who has been wrongfully dismissed may bring an action for damages against his former employer representing the amount of wages owed to him in respect of work already done and in respect of wages that the employee would have earned had he been given the amount of notice to which he was entitled. The amount of wages lost is determined by the ordinary principles of common law and includes all sums connected with the job, such as loss of tips etc. Damages for wrongful dismissal cannot normally include compensation for injured feelings or pride or the fact that future earnings may be affected. The object of damages is to compensate the injured party for what he actually lost, not to punish the party in breach of contract, and therefore the courts have developed principles to ensure that the employee who has been wrongfully dismissed receives compensation only for his actual loss.

Damages against employee

Where an employee fails to give sufficient notice to his employer, the employer may sue the employee for damages representing the loss, which follows from the breach of contract. In practice, such actions are infrequent because the loss is often minimal.

Specific performance

Specific performance is an order from the court directing that the parties to a contract perform their contractual obligations. It is a fundamental principle of labour law that specific performance is granted to compel performance of a contract of employment and this principle is now embodied in s 235 of the Trade Union and Labour Relations (Consolidation) Act 1992.

Injunction

An injunction is an order from a court forbidding certain conduct, e.g. the breaking of a term of the contract of employment. Hence it may be used to prevent a breach of a covenant restraining an employee from taking employment with a rival of his former employer. The courts usually refuse to grant an injunction if it compels performance.

By virtue of the Trade Union and Labour Relations Act 1992, no court may issue an injunction if the effect of such an order would be to compel an employee to do any work or to attend any place to work.

However, where the injunction compelling performance is to the benefit of the employee, the court may be prepared to grant such an order. In Hill v CA Parsons LTD (1972) the defendant employers wished to enter into an agreement with an organisation of workers whereby it was agreed that all employers in certain sections, including the plaintiff, would be obliged to join that organisation.

This arrangement was legal at the time but under the Industrial Relations Act 1971 it would have been invalid. The plaintiff did not wish to join the organisation and he was dismissed with four weeks notice. The Court of Appeal held that he was wrongfully dismissed since he was entitled to at least six months notice and furthermore an injunction was awarded which prevented the employee from being dismissed until that time elapsed by which time he would have a remedy under the 1971 Act.

Declaration

A declaration is an order from the court, which simply determines the rights of the parties in the case. It has no binding force in itself and is not available to all employees being restricted to those persons whose employment is derived from statute.

Written statement of reasons for dismissal

An employee who has been continuously employed for at least a year (2 years after April 2012) and who has been dismissed, subject to the statutory provisions of the 2002 Act and the following of a formal procedure, is entitled to receive, upon request, a written statement of the reasons for his dismissal. The employer must supply the reason in writing within 14 days of the request. A claim may be presented to an industrial tribunal by an employee that his employer has "unreasonably" refused to provide a written statement of the reasons for dismissal or that it is inadequate or untrue. The right to a written statement only arises where the employee has been dismissed by his employer.

Suspension

In accordance with the general principle that an employer fulfils his contractual obligations by paying wages in accordance with the contract of employment, he may suspend an employee on full wages without breach of contract. An employer may only suspend an employee without pay if the contract expressly or impliedly provided for this. If the contract does not so provide, it is a breach of contract. Therefore, an employee who is suspended without contractual authority may treat himself as dismissed and claim accordingly.

Unfair Dismissal

The present law relating to unfair dismissal is to be found in the Employment Rights Act 1996. The significance of the concept of unfair dismissal is that it represents a further, and most important, step towards recognising the property right, which an employee has in his job. Additionally, it is no longer possible for an employer to end a contract by simply giving notice and thereby totally discharging his responsibilities. The threat of dismissal is no longer quite so important since the employee has a remedy if the threat is implemented. The 1996 Act provides that, subject to certain specified exceptions, every employee has the right not to be unfairly dismissed. It should be noted that a complaint of unfair dismissal does not depend upon the employer having acted in breach of contract but simply that the employer has terminated the contract in circumstances which are unfair.

Certain categories of employees are excluded: employees who, at the effective date of termination of the contract have been continuously employed for less than one year, *two years if employed after 6th April 2012,* persons over retiring age, persons employed in the police service, share fishermen, employees who ordinarily work outside Great Britain, employees employed on fixed term contracts and persons covered by a designated dismissals procedure agreement.

Dismissal

If an action for unfair dismissal is to succeed, the employee must first establish that he was dismissed within the meaning of the Act. The employee must establish constructive dismissal if alleged.

The Act provides that:

"an employee shall be treated as dismissed by his employer if the contract under which he is employed by the employer is terminated by the employer whether it is so terminated by notice or without notice or where under that contract he is employed for a fixed term, that term expires without being renewed under the same contract or the employee terminates that contract, with or without notice, in circumstances such that he is entitled to terminate it without notice by reason of the employers conduct".

The Act refers to the concept of so-called "constructive' dismissal. If an employee leaves employment entirely voluntarily, there is no dismissal but if he leaves because of the employers conduct then it may be deemed "constructive".

The courts and tribunals have been concerned to define the circumstances in which an employee is entitled to regard himself as having been constructively dismissed. In Western Excavating LTD v Sharp (1978) the tribunals found that sufficiently unreasonable behaviour on the part of the employer entitled an employee to leave his job and claim constructive dismissal. However, the Court of Appeal rejected the unreasonableness test and established that the correct test is one based on strict contractual principles. Accordingly, an employee is only able successfully to argue constructive dismissal where the employer has breached the contract in such a way as to justify the employee in treating himself as discharged from further performance. The action of an employer may involve breach of an express or implied term.

When is dismissal unfair?

The expression "unfair dismissal" is in no sense a commonsense expression capable of being understood by the person in the street. Whether a dismissal is unfair is affected, but not conclusively determined, by whether one or both parties has broken the terms of the contract of employment. The employer cannot, in seeking to show that a dismissal was not unfair rely on alleged misconduct not known to him at the time of the dismissal. An otherwise fair dismissal is not automatically rendered unfair by a failure to give proper notice.

Reasonableness. It is for the employer to establish the reason for the dismissal. The tribunal must then satisfy itself as to whether the employer acted reasonably or unreasonably. The EAT laid down the following general principles in Iceland Frozen Foods v Jones (1982):

a) In applying the provisions of the 1996 Act a tribunal must consider the reasonableness of the employers conduct and not simply whether they (the members of the tribunal) consider the dismissal unfair.

b) In judging the reasonableness of the employer's conduct a tribunal must not substitute its own decision as to what was the right course to adopt for that of the employer.

c) In many cases there is a band of reasonable responses to the employees conduct within which one employer might take one view and another quite reasonably another.

d) The function of the tribunal is to determine whether in the particular circumstances the decision to dismiss fell within the band of reasonable responses, which a reasonable employer might have adopted. If the dismissal falls within the band it is fair. If it falls outside the band it is unfair.

In deciding whether an employer acted reasonably, the industrial tribunal is required to have regard to the provisions of the ACAS Code of Practice-Disciplinary Code of Practice and Procedures in Employment. In broad terms, this provides that the disciplinary rules and procedures ought to have been made known to each employee and that a disciplinary procedure ought to contain certain essential procedures.

Reasons for dismissal

There are five categories of reasons, which, if one is established by the employer, may make the dismissal fair provided that the tribunal is satisfied that the employer acted reasonably.

These are as follows:

a) Capability or qualification

b) Conduct

c) Redundancy

d) Illegality of continued employment

e) Some other substantial reason.

In addition, an employer in certain circumstances, can dismiss an employee for reasons connected to pregnancy. Usually, it is automatically unfair to do so unless the employer can establish that at the effective date of termination, because of her pregnancy, she:

a) is or will have become incapable of adequately doing the work she is employed to do or: or

b) cannot or will not be able to do the work she is employed to do without a contravention (either by her or her employer) of a duty of restriction imposed by law.

154

In Brown v Stockton on Tees Borough Council (1988) the House of Lords (Supreme Court) held that if a woman was selected for redundancy because she is pregnant, such a dismissal is automatically unfair. Indeed, Lord Griffith stated that "it surely cannot have been intended that an employer should be entitled to take advantage of a redundancy situation to weed out his pregnant employer".

However, even where the circumstances of a and b above apply, the dismissal is still unfair if the employer has a suitable vacancy, i.e. appropriate for a pregnant woman to do and not substantially less favourable than her existing employment in relation to the nature, terms and place of employment, which he fails to offer her.

Dismissal for trade union reasons

References in this section are to the Trade Union and Labour Relations (Consolidation) Act 1992. Trade Union membership or activities. Except in exceptional cases, a dismissal is automatically unfair if the employee can establish that the principal reason for it was that the employer was, or proposed to become, a member of an independent trade union, or that the employee had taken or proposed to take part in the activities of an independent trade union at any appropriate time or that the employee was not a member of any or a particular trade union, or had refused or proposed to refuse to become or remain a member.

Other reasons for dismissal

An industrial tribunal cannot determine whether a dismissal was fair or unfair if it is known that at the date of dismissal the employer was conducting or instituting a lock out or the complainant was taking part in a strike or other industrial action, unless it is shown:

a) that one or more relevant employees of the same employer have not been dismissed: or
b) that any such employee has, before the expiry of the period of three months

beginning with the employee's date of dismissal, been offered re-engagement and that the complainant has not been offered re-engagement.

National security

If an employee has shown to have been dismissed on grounds of national security, as evidenced by a certificate signed by or on behalf of a minister of the Crown, the tribunal must dismiss the complaint.

In Council of Civil Service Unions v Minister for the Civil Service (1985) (the GCHQ case), the court held that the requirements of national security outweighed those of fairness when the minister decided to ban trade unions at GCHQ, without consultation with the trade unions. Workers who refused to give up their trade union membership were subsequently fairly dismissed.

Procedure

An employee who considers that he has been unfairly dismissed may present a complaint to the Central Office of Industrial Tribunals within three months of the effective date of termination or within such further period as the tribunal considers reasonable in a case where it is satisfied that it was not reasonably practicable for the complaint to be presented within a time period of three months. Where the dismissal is unfair (failure to offer re-engagement where the dismissal is connected with a lockout or strike) the time limit is six months from the date of dismissal. A copy of the application is sent to the employer as respondent. If the employer wishes to contest any aspect of the complaint, he must enter a "notice of appearance" within 14 days, although tribunals have a wide discretion to grant an extension of time. Once this has happened, a date is set down for the hearing of the case by an industrial tribunal.

Conciliation

A copy of the application is also sent to a conciliation officer. He is under a statutory duty, either at the request of the parties or on his own initiative, to endeavor to promote a voluntary settlement of the issue, either by way of an agreement to reinstate or re-engage the complainant or an agreement as to the payment of compensation in respect of the dismissal. there is no legal duty upon the parties to co-operate with the conciliation officer.

Pre-hearing Assessments

Under the Industrial Tribunals Regulations (S1 1985/16) provision is made for a pre-hearing assessment of the case to be made at the request of either of the parties or on the notion of the tribunal itself. At the tribunal, it is for the complainant to establish that he was dismissed (unless dismissal is conceded). It is then for the tribunal to satisfy itself as to whether the dismissal was fair or unfair in accordance with the principles stated above.

If the dismissal is found to be unfair, the tribunal will consider the remedies, which may be awarded. An appeal, on a point of law only, lies from an industrial tribunal to the Employment Appeal Tribunal.

Remedies

Reinstatement and re-engagement orders. If the Tribunal finds the dismissal unfair, it must explain to the complainant the remedies available and ask if he wishes to be reinstated or re-engaged. If the employee indicates that this is his wish then the Tribunal must consider whether it is practicable for the employer to comply with such an order. If the employer complies, but not fully, with a reinstatement or re-engagement order then, unless the tribunal is satisfied that it was not practicable to comply with the order, an additional award of compensation must be made. If a reinstatement or re-engagement order is made but not complied with at all or if no such order is made, the tribunal must make an award of compensation

****

3.3

DISCRIMINATION IN THE WORKPLACE

The ability of employers to discriminate in the workplace has been steadily eroded. In 2010, the Equality Act came onto the statute books and was implemented in two stages, October 2010 and April 2011. The Act replaced nine previous pieces of legislation, bringing them all under one umbrella.

The main changes contained within the Equality Act 2010 are making pay secrecy gagging clauses unenforceable, putting restrictions on employers asking job applicants questions about disability or health, making employers responsible for protecting their staff from harassment by customers and allowing employment tribunals that find an employer has discriminated against an employee to make recommendations that could affect the whole workforce.

The Equality Act replaced the Equal Pay Act 1970, The Sex Discrimination Act 1975, the Race Relations Act 1976, The Disability Discrimination Act 1996, The Employment Equality (Sexual Orientation) Regulations 2003, The Employment equality (Religion or Belief) Regulations 2003 and the Employment Equality (Age) Regulations 2006, the Equality Act 2006 and the Equality Act (Sexual Orientation) Regulations 2007. In most cases, the thrust of the Acts that were incorporated into the Equality Act 2010 have remained unchanged, but are now contained within the new legislation. Outlined below are the main points of the Acts.

Equal Pay
In broad terms, the Equal Pay Act 1970, which has now been replaced wholesale by the Equality Act 2010, was concerned with less favourable treatment of one person relative to another in respect of matters governed by the contract under which a person is employed whereas the Sex

Discrimination act 1975 dealt with less favourable treatment in matters not governed by the contract, on grounds of sex and/or marital status.

The Equal Pay Act 1970 was influenced by the treaty of Rome and the effect of certain European Community Directives have been considerable in this area and have significant practical consequences for any applicant contemplating bringing an action alleging breach of the Equality Act 2010.

Article 119 of the Treaty of Rome provides that: "each member state shall maintain the application of the principle that men and women should receive equal pay for equal work. For the purpose of this article, pay means the ordinary basic or minimum wage or salary and any other consideration, whether in cash or kind, which the worker receives, directly or indirectly in respect of his employment from his employer. The Article is directly enforceable by individuals in the courts of member states of the EEC. The 2002 Employment Rights Act introduced the right of the employee to give the employer a questionnaire in order to ascertain whether or not the employer is actually paying and treating equally. The employer does not have to comply.

Sex Discrimination Act 1975

This Act has also been replaced wholesale by the Equality Act 2010. In relation to employment, the Sex Discrimination Act was intended to render discrimination on the grounds of sex and/or the fact that a person is married unlawful as regards those areas of employment not dealt with by the terms of the contract. The Act rendered discrimination on the above grounds unlawful except in the following cases:

a) Discrimination by way of special treatment afforded to women in connection with pregnancy or childbirth.

b) Where in the previous year there were no or few members of one sex doing a particular job, certain discrimination in favour of members of that sex is allowed.

c) Discrimination in the selection, promotion or training of a person is permissible where being a man or woman is a genuine occupational qualification.

160

d) There are special rules relating to the police, prison officers and ministers of religion.

e) There are special rules relating to death or retirement. The position here had been much influenced by community law which in turn led to the amendment of the Sex Discrimination Act 1986. Under Community law it is quite clear that the domestic legislation of a member state may fix discriminatory retirement ages.

Section 6 of the Act provided that the following areas of employment are within the scope of the act.

a) Arrangements for selecting of employees and making offers of employment.

b) The terms upon which employment is offered but not the terms themselves when employment has been obtained, this latter matter being within the scope of the Equality Act 2010.

c) Access to promotion, training, transfer or any other benefit, facilities or services.

d) Dismissal or the subjecting of a person to any other detriment, e.g., suspension from work.

It is unlawful to publish, or cause to be published an advertisement which indicates, or might reasonably indicate, an intention to do an act which was contrary to the Act.

The meaning of discrimination. The Act embodied three kinds of discrimination, direct discrimination unfavourable treatment on grounds of race, sex etc. Indirect discrimination-this is where the complainant must demonstrate that the employer applies a requirement or condition which he applies or would apply to members of the other sex/single persons. That it is to the complainants detriment because he or she cannot comply with it.

An example of the operation of this provision would be where an employer requires all his employees to be over six feet tall. This could only be justified if the employer could demonstrate that the job demanded it.

One important case in this area is Price v Civil Service Commission (1978) Held: a civil service condition that candidates for certain posts should be no more than 28 years of age was indirect discrimination because women in their late twenties were frequently occupied in having and rearing children.

Discrimination by victimisation. S 4, this dealt with discrimination against a person who has brought proceedings, given evidence, information, alleged a contravention etc under the Sex Discrimination Act or Equal Pay Act. Such a person must not be treated less favourably by the alleged discriminator than another person in those circumstances was or would be treated.

In relation to discrimination on grounds of sex (as opposed to discrimination against married persons) s7 provides that certain kinds of employment are excluded from the operation of the Act, namely where being a member of one sex is a "genuine occupational qualification" for the job. Two general points should be noted:

a) These provisions do not apply to the terms upon which employment is offered, dismissal or subjecting a person to any other detriment.

b) These provisions do not apply to the filling of a vacancy where the employer already has male (or female) employees capable of filling it and whom it would be reasonable to employ on those duties and whose numbers are sufficient to meet the employer's likely requirements without undue inconvenience.

Being a man or woman is a genuine occupational qualification for a job where the essential nature of the job calls for a man for reasons of physiology or authenticity e.g. actors, models etc. In addition where the job needs to be held by a man to preserve decency or privacy or the job is likely to involve the holder doing work or living in a private home and needs to be held by a same sex person because objections might be raised to a member of the opposite sex in attendance. Also, the nature or the location of the establishment effectively requires the employee to live in and in the absence of separate sleeping accommodation and sanitary facilities, it is not reasonable to expect the employer to provide such things. In addition, the nature of the establishment where the work is done, i.e. a hospital or prison requires that the job be done by a man.

Sexual Orientation

The Court of Appeal in R v Ministry of Defence Ex p Smith (1996) stated that sex discrimination legislation was aimed at gender discrimination not orientation discrimination. However, from December 2003 the position became clearer with the introduction of the Employment Equality (Sexual Orientation) Regulations 2003 (now replaced by the Equality Act 2010), which gave effect to the EU Directive on discrimination and which makes both direct and indirect discrimination on the grounds of sexual orientation unlawful. The law concerning transsexuals, those who have undergone or intend to undergo gender realignment has also been covered by legislation, the relevant legislation being The Sex Discrimination (Gender Reassignment) Regulations 1999 (Now replaced by the Equality Act 2010) which amended the Sex Discrimination Act to specifically include discrimination on the grounds of gender reassignment.

Race Relations Act 1976

The 1976 Act, now replaced in full by the Equality Act 2010, was concerned with discrimination on grounds of colour, race, nationality, or ethnic or national origin. Some difficulty has been experienced over the question of the meaning of ethnic origin and in particular its relationship with race.

An important defining case in this respect was Mandla v Lee (1983). The House of Lords resolved the matter. The question was whether Sikhs are a group of persons defined by ethnic origin so as to fall within the protection of the Act. It was held that Sikhs did constitute an ethnic group. "Ethnic" was used in the Act in a sense much wider than that of "race" and an ethnic group can be identified by some or all of such essential factors as a long history, cultural tradition, common geographical origin, common language and a common religion.

It should be noted that a racial group cannot be defined by the factor of language alone.

The 1976 Act was concerned not only with employment but covers such things as the provision of services, housing etc. There are a number of exceptions to the 1976 Act including where being of a certain race etc is deemed to be a genuine occupational qualification, such as specific providers of services to defined communities.

Discrimination on the grounds of disability

In 1995 the Disability Discrimination Act was passed. This has now been replaced wholesale with the 2010 Equality Act. In relation to employment, it made all employers of over 20 employees or more legally liable for discrimination against disabled people. Part 11 of the Act, relating to employment, came into force at the end of 1996 at which time a code of practice came into in force to help on interpretation. To be protected against discrimination an individual must be a person who has a disability or had a disability. Disability is defined as physical or mental impairment, which has a substantial and long-term effect on the person's ability to carry out day-to-day activities.

In relation to employment the individual is protected against discrimination. It should be noted that the Act only mentioned discrimination on the grounds of disability and thus, unlike the Race Relations Act and Sex Discrimination Act allowed an employer to positively discriminate in the case of a person with a disability.

The Act, in s 4 outlines acts of discrimination. These principally cover the arrangements for appointing employees, the terms on which employment is offered and refusal of employment. It is also unlawful to discriminate in the terms of employment, in the opportunities offered for training, promotion, transfer or any other benefit or to dismiss a person because of disability.

Age discrimination in the workplace

On 1st October 2006, The Employment Equality (Age) Regulations (EE(A) Regs) took effect, outlawing age discrimination in both the workplace and vocational training. These Regulations have now been replaced wholesale by the Equality Act 2010. It is against the law to treat a person unfairly at work because of age. It is against the law to discriminate for being too young or old. The law only covers work, adult education and training. The law applies to a person whether working or applying for a job. It is against the law to bully or make offensive comments in the workplace because of age. There are some exceptions to the general rule. For example, an employer may occasionally be allowed to discriminate against someone because of their age but only if they can show that this is justified. An employer may argue that it doesn't make business sense to employ someone over 60 years of age if there is a long and involved period of training allied to the job.

Retirement and age discrimination

The normal retirement age for both men and women is 65, unless the employment contract states that it is higher. An employer was allowed to force a person to retire at the normal retirement age. However, with the scrapping of the Default Retirement Age between April and October 2011, employers will no longer be able to force employees to retire at 65.

Job applications and discrimination

It is generally against the law for employers to refuse to take a person on or promote because of age. In most cases employers shouldn't target adverts at specific age groups. There are some exceptions to this rule.

Unfair dismissal

It is discriminatory to dismiss a person because of age. A claim for unfair dismissal may be made if this has been the case.

****

Ch. 4

BUSINESS LAW-COMPANY LAW

When people set up a business they will usually form a (limited) company or a partnership. The main distinction between a company and a partnership is that the company is treated as a separate entity, or person in law. The partnership, on the other hand is not seen as a separate entity and consists only of those who have chosen to join together for business purposes.

One other crucial distinction is that a company will pay corporation tax, whilst a partnership will pay only that tax due as an individual liability.

A company has access to what is known as "limited liability". This is where the liability for debt of directors is limited. Not all companies are limited companies. If a company is not limited there is no requirement to file accounts at Companies House. Partnerships have no such access to limited liability.

A company can separate ownership from control. People who subscribe to a company and purchase its shares do not necessarily have any control over the company or a hand in running the business. This is especially the case in a large Public Limited Company, where shareholders receive a return on their investment in the company.

A further distinction and advantage for a company is in the area of raising finance. The company as a separate entity can raise finance in its own right, mortgage any assets by way of a floating charge, and generally enjoy access to finance that is not available to a partnership.

Public companies and private companies

Another main area which runs through company law is that of the distinction between the public company and the private company. The majority of companies in the United Kingdom are private companies. One main feature of company law is that, with a few exceptions, the same rules apply to private companies as to public companies.

The second EC directive on company law did, however, lead to modifications to company law, with distinctions being drawn between public and private companies, these being incorporated into the Companies Act 2006.

One main feature of a public company is that it must have a minimum subscribed share capital of at least £50,000, or its equivalent in Euros paid up to at least 25 percent before it can be incorporated (s586 of the CA 2006). The second EC directive sets out the regulations for this, with the minimum subscribed share capital for public companies within the EU being £25,000 ECU. In addition to the payment of the minimum subscribed share capital to at least 25 percent on initial allotment of shares, the whole of any premium must be paid up.

A further distinction between public and private companies is in the name of the company. The Companies Act of 2006 states that a public company must end with suffix "public limited company" or the abbreviation PLC. In Wales the term is cwmni cyhoeddus cyfyngedig with the abbreviation ccc. A private company will end with the term "limited" or the Welsh equivalent cyfyngedig or "cyf".

In addition, another fundamental distinction between the public and private company is that the private company is prohibited from seeking finance from the public by offering shares or debentures. The public company is authorised to seek shares in this way.

Company limited by guarantee

A company limited by guarantee is a private company, very like a private company limited by shares, but it does not have a share capital. It is widely used for charities, clubs, community enterprises and some co-operatives. The vast majority of such companies are non-profit distributing, but they do not have to be.

A company limited by guarantee is registered at Companies House, has articles of association, directors, etc., and is subject to all the requirements of the Companies Acts (except those relating to shares). There are no shares and so no shareholders, but such a company does have members, who meet and control the company through general meetings. The directors are often called a management committee or council of management, etc. but in law are still company directors and subject to all the rules that affect other directors.

A company limited by guarantee confers limited liability as effectively as a company limited by shares. The articles state that the members guarantee to pay its debts, but only up to a fixed amount each. Usually that sum is £1, and no member can be liable for more than that amount if the company fails. The Companies Act 2006 also outlines other distinctions between companies:

- A private company can operate with one director, in contrast to the public company which is required to have two

- A private company needs only to have one member whereas a public company has to have two (s154 CA 2006).

- The company secretary of a private company can be anyone and that person needs no particular qualifications. There is now no legal requirement for a company secretary of a private company under the CA 2006. The company secretary of a public company must be qualified, holding a recognised qualification in this area in order to hold the post.

- Before a public company can pay a dividend, it must ensure that it has trading profits and that its capital assets are maintained in value to at least the value of the subscribed share capital plus undistributable reserves. There is no such rule applying to a private company (CA 2006)

- Before a public company can distribute shares in exchange for property it must obtain an independent experts valuation of the property. This requirement does not apply to a private company (CA 2006)

- A public company may not issue shares in exchange for services. This rule does not apply to a private company (CA 2006).

- The Directors of a public company must call an Extraordinary General Meeting (EGM) if it suffers a serious loss of capital. There is no requirement for a private company to do this.

- Proxies in a private company may speak at a meeting. In a public company there is no such right.

- In a private company, there are courses of action, which may be taken in order to dispense with formalities such as the need to hold an Annual General Meeting, the laying of accounts and the annual appointment of auditors. This is not the case with a public company, which is rigidly bound.

- Private companies may act by unanimous written resolution, in most cases. This does not apply to public companies.

- Where there is a proposal to elect a director aged 70 or over to the board of a public company, special notice is required. There is no such requirement for a private company.

- The minimum age for a company director under the CA 2006 s 157, for both private and public companies is 16.

Limited Liability Partnerships

Under the Limited Liability Partnerships Act 2000, it is possible to create a different form of business association called a limited liability partnership. Under the LLPA 2000, a LLP becomes a corporate body with a legal personality separate from that of its members. It follows therefore that members of a LLP will not normally become liable for the debts of the LLP. The law relating to ordinary partnerships does not relate to a LLP.

Many of the detailed provisions relating to LLP's are to be found in secondary legislation, in particular the Limited Partnership Regulations 2001. These regulations apply some of the provisions of the CA 2006 and the Insolvency Act 1986 to LLP's with some modifications to reflect the different nature of an LLP.

Formation of an LLP

An LLP is created by registration with the registrar of companies. Once the registrar has registered an LLP and issued a certificate of incorporation, a new corporate body with a separate legal personality of its own is created. Section 2 (1) of the LPA 2000 provides that:

Two or more persons associated for carrying on a lawful business with a view to profit must have subscribed their names to an incorporation document which is to be delivered to the registrar of companies.

Community Interest Companies

The Companies (Audit, Investigations and Community Enterprise) Act 2004 and regulations made under the Act, establish the legislative framework for CICs. CICs are regulated by the CIC Regulator.

A Community Interest Company can be registered in England and Wales, Scotland or Northern Ireland. It is a hybrid between a charity and a profit making company. A Community Interest Company must be set up and run for the benefit of the community. A CIC can only be registered with the consent of the Community Interest Companies Regulator. The application must comply with CIC legislation as well as the usual rules for registration of a company. The CIC Regulator has to be satisfied that the proposed company is being set up to benefit the community and that its articles include all the provisions required of a community interest company. Each year, the CIC must submit a return stating what its activities have been and that these have been of community benefit.

Property management companies

A property management company in England and Wales, Scotland or Northern Ireland is a particular type of company: one set up to hold an interest in a property which is divided into units, each unit being owned separately. A typical example is a large house which has been divided into a number of flats (sometimes called a flat management company), each flat being owned by one or two people. Such a company can also be used for large blocks of flats, housing estates and commercial properties divided into units. A property management company will always be a private limited company. It may be limited by shares or limited by guarantee. People who deal with property management companies professionally tend to have their preferences. It is one of those circumstances where either type of company will work perfectly well. The only significant difference between them is that a company limited by shares has a share capital, owned by its shareholders and a company limited by guarantee does not, but is controlled by its shareholders. If the company is to own the freehold, some people prefer it to be a company limited by shares as this gives a form of ownership between the shareholders (who own the company) and the property (which is owned by the company). On the other hand, with a company limited by guarantee, there is no need to transfer a share when the flat is sold.

The concept of the corporate personality

The principle of the separate legal personality of a company was established in an important case, Saloman v A Saloman (1897). The facts of the case were that Saloman had incorporated his shoe repair business, transferring it to a company. He took all the shares of the company with the exception of six which were held by his wife, daughter and four sons. Part of the payment for transfer of the business was made in the form of debentures (secured loan) issued by the company to Saloman. Saloman transferred the debentures to Broderip in exchange for a loan. Saloman defaulted on payment of interest on the loan and Broderip sought to enforce the security against the company. Unsecured creditors tried to put the company into liquidation. There was a dispute between Broderip and the unsecured creditors over who had priority over payment of the debt. It was argued for the creditors that Salmons security was void as the company was a sham and was in reality the agent of Salomon.

The House of Lords held that this was not the case as the company had been properly incorporated and therefore the security was valid and could be enforced. This case is seen as one of the most important cases in company law as it is from this that many principles of company law flow. There are certain statutory exceptions to the Salmon principle and they are as follows:

- Section 7 of the Companies Act 2006 provides that if the membership of a public company falls below the statutory minimum of two then the remaining member should after a period of six months grace, be liable for the company's debts and obligations where he or she knew of the situation.

- Section 767 (3) of the Companies Act 2006 provides that where a public company fails to obtain a trading certificate in addition to its certificate of incorporation before trading and borrowing money then the companies directors are liable for any obligations incurred.

- Sections 398-408 of the Companies Act 2006 provides that where a group situation exists (i.e. where there is a holding company and subsidiaries) then group accounts should be prepared. In assessing whether this is the case, clearly the veil is being lifted to see if the holding company/subsidiary relationship exists.

- Section 83 of the Companies Act 2006 provides that if a company officer misdescribes the company in a letter, bill, invoice, order, receipt or any other document then the officer is liable in the event of the obligation not being honored.

- Section 994 of the Companies Act 2006 may involve lifting the veil to determine, for example, the basis on which the company was formed.

- Sections 1159-1160 of the Companies Act 2006 set out the formula for determining if a holding company/subsidiary company relationship exists.

- Section 15 of the Company Directors Disqualification Act 1986 provides that if a director who is disqualified continues to act, he or she will be personally liable for the debts and obligations of the company.

- Section 122 (1) (g) of the Insolvency Act 1986 provides that a petitioner may present a petition to wind up a company on the just and equitable ground.

- On occasion, this may be based on a situation involving the lifting of the company veil in order to determine the basis of the company formation.

- Section 213 of the Insolvency Act 1986 provides that where a person trades through the medium of a company, knowing that the company is unable to pay its debts, he or she may be held liable for contributions to the companies assets where the company is being wound up. This has a criminal counterpart in s999 (1) of the CA 2006.

- Section 6 of the Law of Property Act 1969 provides that where a person has a controlling interest in a company which is carrying on a business, the business is treated as the controller for the purposes of refusing a renewal of a tenancy issued out of the Landlord and Tenant Act 1954.

In addition to the statutory exceptions to the Salomon principle there are certain judicial decisions which have had an impact. One such decision is that of combating fraud. There are several well-known legal cases that have dealt with fraud.

One such case is that of Jones v Lipman (1962) where a vendor decided to sell a piece of land and then changed his mind. This resulted in the would-be purchaser suing for specific performance. In order to avoid this, the vendor transferred the piece of land to a company. The courts held that although the company was another legal entity nevertheless the action was designed to avoid legal action and the courts refused to accept the action of transferring the land and ordered specific performance against the vendor.

Therefore the action of transferring assets from the individual to a company in order to change a legal status is not tolerated if it is seen as fraudulent, as in the case above. There are numerous other examples of a company veil being lifted in order to combat fraud.

Group structures

Group structures are governed by s1159 of the CA 2006. Sometimes the fact that a company is within a group is seen as a reason for identifying it with another company within the group. In Harold Holdsworth and Co (Wakefield) Ltd v Caddies (1955) the respondent held an employment contract with the appellant company to serve it as managing director. The House of Lords held that the appellant company could require the respondent to serve a subsidiary company.

A fundamental case in this area is DHN Food Distributors Ltd v Tower Hamlets London Borough Council (1976). This case concerned compensation for compulsory purchase. The company operating the business was the holding company and the premises were owned by the companies wholly owned subsidiary. Compensation was only payable for disturbance to the companies business if the business was operated on land owned by the company.

In this case, Lord Denning said:

"In many respects a group of companies are treated together for the purposes of accounts, they are treated as one concern. This is especially the case when a parent company owns all the shares of the subsidiary-so much so that it can control the activities of the subsidiaries. These subsidiaries are bound hand and foot and must do just what the parent company says."

Companies and crimes and negligence

Companies, as any individual, can commit crimes, although there are certain obvious exceptions, such as rape or murder. A company can, however, commit manslaughter. In December 1994, OLL Limited became the first company in England to be convicted of manslaughter. This arose from the death of four young people in a canoeing accident in Lyme Bay which was organised by the company.

In the case, Kite v OLL Ltd 1994, the managing director of the company that organised the trip was imprisoned for manslaughter and the company fined £60,000.

The Law Commission reported on the law of corporate manslaughter in consultation paper no 135 (1994). They recommended a new offence based on whether the companies conduct fell significantly below what could reasonably be expected of it in the context of the significant risk of death or injury of which it should have been aware. In a later report (Law Commission Paper no 237) Legislating the Criminal Code, Involuntary Manslaughter (1996) the Law Commission, in its final report, called for a new offence of corporate killing comparable to killing by gross negligence.

It is imperative that at least one person should be recognised and identified as the directing force of the company causing death by gross negligence when acting as the company.

In the only other case of a company being convicted of manslaughter, Jackson Transport (Ossett) Ltd. The company concerned was a medium sized company employing about 40 people. A person was killed in May 1994 while he was cleaning behind a tanker containing chemicals. Mr Jackson, the owner, ran the business himself and he and the company was convicted of manslaughter.

Companies may also commit strict liability offences. This is important in areas such as pollution and food safety. There is however, a diligence defence and if the company can demonstrate the practice of diligence, or that lack of diligence was on the part of a person who was not the true embodiment of the company, it will escape liability.

****

4.2

THE CONSTITUTION OF A COMPANY

Under the Companies Act 2006, the importance of a company's memorandum of association has been reduced to a mere historical record. Constitutional provisions are to be contained within the Articles of Association instead. The memorandum is a document that needs to be submitted as part of the incorporation process and will not be capable of amendment. The information that was contained within the memorandum will now be provided to the registrar in an application for registration under s 9 of the Companies Act 2006.

The application for registration must contain the following::

- The name of the company (s9) (2) of the Companies Act 2006.
- If the company is a public company a statement indicating this s 9(2).
- A statement that the registered office of the company is situated in England and Wales, in Wales or in Scotland s9 (7).

The application must also contain:

- A statement of initial shareholding
- A Statement of share capital
- A Statement of guarantee
- A Statement of proposed officers
- A Statement of compliance

Objects clauses and *ultra vires*

This is an area that has been amended by the introduction of the CA 2006. Now, by virtue of s 31 of the CA 2006 unless a company's articles specifically restrict the objects of the company, its objects are unrestricted. If the company does decide to amend its objects, then this change must be made by amendment to the articles. The new law is stated in s 40 of the CA 2006. The effect of the new law is to effectively abolish *ultra vires*. However, there are still occasions where a challenge could arise. These are where a director or connected person is involved or a third party acted in bad faith. A Challenge could also arise if an injunction is sought to prevent directors acting or to allege a breach of duty after events. S 239 of the CA 2006 now only requires ordinary resolutions to ratify any breaches of duty by directors. However, the votes of any director or person involved in the breach of duty will not count. S 41 (3) of the CA 2006 makes any directors involved liable to account for the transaction and to indemnify the company whether they knew they were exceeding their powers or not.

The position at common law

The old case will still be applicable in certain limited circumstances. Prior to statutory reform, at common law, contracts that were outside the scope of the company's objects were held to be *ultra vires* and void. Before statutory intervention therefore the question was simple: if the objects clause covered the relevant contract it was valid. If it was outside the scope of the company's permitted range of activities it was void and unenforceable. There are several cases which serve to highlight the nature of the above. One such case is that of Payne and Co Ltd (1904) where a company borrowed money which was then used for purposes outside of the objects of the company. The lender was able to enforce the loan because he did not know the purpose of the loan.

In Re John Beauforte Ltd (1953) a different decision was reached on the basis that a supplier to the company provided coke. The company could have been using the coke for internal purposes as it was engaged in the manufacturer of veneered panels. The order was placed on notepaper showing that the company was engaged in this business and the courts held that the combination of constructive notice of what the company could do and the actual notice of what it was doing was fatal to the suppliers claim.

Statutory intervention

Article 9 of the first EC directive on company law provided as follows:

- Acts done by the organs of the company shall be binding upon it even if those acts are not within the objects of the company, unless such acts exceed powers that the law confers or allows to be conferred on those organs.

Since that first article, company law has developed and now the Companies Act 2006 has amended the law on ultra vires and objects clauses.

The Prentice Report (reform of the ultra vires rule, a consultative document (1986) (par 50) put forward the following recommendations in relation to the reform of the ultra vires rule:

- A company should have the capacity to do any act whatsoever
- A third party dealing with the company should not be affected by the contents of any document merely because it is registered with the registrar of companies or with the company.
- A company should be bound by the acts of its board or an individual director.
- The third party should be under no obligation to determine the scope of the authority of a company's board or individual director, or the contents of the company's articles or memorandum.
- A third party who has actual knowledge that a board or an individual director do not possess the authority to enter into a transaction on behalf of the company should not be allowed to enforce against the company but the company should be free to ratify this. The same result should obtain where a third party has knowledge that the transaction falls outside of the company's objects, but in this case ratification should be by a special resolution.

- Knowledge in this context will require understanding, and it will only be the knowledge of the individual entering into the particular transaction that will be relevant
- The proposal (in relation to third parties) should be modified where a third party is an officer or director of the company and in this situation constructive knowledge should be sufficient to render the transaction unenforceable and for this purpose constructive knowledge should mean the type of knowledge which may reasonably be expected of a person carrying out the functions of that director or officer of the company.

In consequence of the recommendations of the Prentice Report the Companies Act of 1989 amended the law on ultra vires and objects clauses.

The Companies act of 2006, provides that the validity of an act done by a company shall not be called into question on the ground of lack of capacity by reason of anything in the company's memorandum. A transaction can thus be enforced by an outsider or the company.

A member may, however, restrain the company from entering into a transaction which is outside the company's objects. This power to restrain the company can only operate where the company has not entered into a binding transaction to perform the act.

If the directors exceed limitations on their powers then they are in breach of their director's duties. Even if the directors conclude a contract outside of the objects clause, and a member has not succeeded in restraining this, the company may be able to sue their directors for breach of duties (Companies Act 2006). It is open to the company to ratify what has been done by special resolution. The company may also ratify by a separate special resolution the breach of the director's duties thereby putting the matter outside of litigation.

S.40 (1) of the CA now provides that where a person deals with a company in good faith the power of the directors to bind the company shall be deemed to be free of any limitation under the company's constitution. The outsider is not to be regarded as in bad faith by reason only by his knowing that the transaction was outside of the director's powers.

Further, this section provides that:

...a party to any transaction with a company is not bound to enquire as to whether it is permitted by the companies memorandum or as to any limitations on the board of directors to bind the company or to authorise others to do so.

The wording under sections s.40 (1) will protect outsiders in most circumstances. The CA 2006 builds on these provisions, which extends to other officers acting on behalf of the company.

This provides that:

... a person shall not be taken to have notice of any such matters merely because of its being disclosed in any document kept by the registrar of companies (and thus available for inspection) or made available by the company for inspection.

The rules governing company names

The first clause in the company's memorandum should be the name of that company. The statutory provisions relating to company names are set out in The Companies Act 2006. These provisions are as follows:

- Section 58 of the CA 2006 provides that the name of a public company must end with the word "PLC" or the Welsh equivalent as mentioned. A private company limited by shares or guarantee should end with "Limited" or the abbreviation Ltd or the Welsh equivalent as mentioned.

- In certain cases, a private limited company may be permitted to omit the word "limited" from the end of its name. The Companies Act 2006 permits companies to omit the word limited on satisfying certain conditions. The company concerned must be a private limited company and have as its objects the promotion of science, commerce, art, education, religion, charity or any profession and anything incidental or conductive to any of these objects and must have a requirement in its constitution that its profits or other income be applied in promoting these objects. The constitution must also prohibit the payment of dividends to its members and require all of the assets which would otherwise be available to its members generally to be transferred on its winding up to another body with similar objects or to a body the objects of which are the promotion of charity and anything incidental.

- Section 53 of the Companies Act 2006 prohibits the use of certain names. The words public limited company, limited and unlimited can only be used at the end of a company name as may be the Welsh equivalents.
- The name must not be the same as a name already registered at Companies House. (s 66 CA 2006)

S 55 of the CA 2006 states that there are certain words and expressions, which require the prior permission of either the Secretary for State or some other designated body.. There is a list of the words specified in regulations made under s55 of the Companies Act. If the name of the company implies some regional, national or international pre-eminence, governmental link or sponsorship or some pre-eminent status, then consent may be required.

- The choice of company name is limited by other considerations. If the name is a registered trademark the person who owns the trademark may take action to prevent the use of the name under the Trades Mark Act 1994.
- The use of a name which is already used by an existing business (whether sole trader, partnership or company) or a name which is similar to that of an existing business such that it appears to the public that there is a link between the two businesses may be subject to legal action, such as an injunction to restrain the company from further use.

Change of name

Section 77 (1) of the Companies Act 2006 provides that a company may change its name by special resolution in general meeting. There are other provisions relating to change of name, that is if the Secretary of State or Companies House gives a direction that the company must do this. This will usually happen in a situation where the original name was misleading or that the name itself is deemed to be of potential harm.

The articles of association of a company

The Articles of association is now the most important document to be submitted to the registrar (CA 2006 s 18). Although a company must have articles of association, the contents of the articles are not laid down by the 2006 CA. Under s 20 of the 2006 CA, a limited company doesn't have to register articles. If they are not registered then model articles (currently being drawn up) will apply. Section 21 of the Companies Act 2006 allows a company to alter its articles by special resolution. However, the power to alter the articles of a company is restricted by the following:

- The company cannot alter its articles in a way which would lead to contravention of the 2006 Companies Act.
- Any alteration of the company's articles which would lead to a difference between, or a clash between the memorandum is void.
- If an alteration of the articles is proposed which conflicts with an order of the court then this would be automatically void.
- If the proposed alteration of the articles leads to an alteration of the class rights then special procedures need to be followed in addition to a special resolution being passed. A company must follow a regime which is appropriate to the variation of class rights which is set out in s121 of the 2006 Companies Act.

If a change of articles involves a variation of class rights then this procedure must be followed. If a company has more than one class of shares then questions of variations of class rights sometimes arise.

Once it has been determined that there is more than one class of share in the company then the next question for determination is whether there has been a variation of rights attached to those shares.

Once it has been established that there has been a variation of class rights then the rules that have to be followed to carry the variation into effect are dependent upon whether the company has a share capital or not. If the company has a share capital then the rights may be varied:

a) in accordance with provision in the company's articles for the variation of those rights; or

b) where the company's articles contain no such provision, if the members of that class consent to the variation in accordance with this section.

The consent required for the purposes of this section on the part of the members of a class is-

a) consent in writing from at least three quarters of the members of the class, or

b) a special resolution passed at a separate general meeting of the members of that class sanctioning the variation.

If class rights are varied, dissentient minorities have special rights to object to the alteration. They must satisfy certain conditions. The dissenters must hold no less than 15% of the issued shares of the class and must not have voted in favour of the resolution (s 633 of the CA 2006). They may then object to the variation within 21 days of consent being given to the resolution.

If the class rights are varied under a procedure set out in the memorandum or articles of association of the company or if the class rights are set out otherwise than in the memorandum or articles are silent on variation, then dissentient minorities have special rights to object to the alteration.

They must satisfy certain conditions:

• The dissenters must hold no less than 15 percent of the issued shares of the class and must not have voted in favour of the resolution. They may then object to the variation within 21 days of the consent being given to the resolution. On occasions, their objections may be upheld by the courts (s 623 CA 2006).

'Bona Fide for the benefit of the company as a whole'

In addition to the various statutory restrictions considered above, the power to alter a company's articles is subject to the overriding principle that any alteration must be bona fide for the benefit of the company as a whole. One case that illustrates this is Allen v Gold Reefs of West Africa Limited.

In this case, the company's articles originally provided:

.....that the company shall have a first and paramount lien for all debts obligations and liabilities of any member to and towards the company upon all shares (not being fully paid) held by such member...........

The alteration proposed was to delete the words 'not being fully paid' to provide the company with a lien over any shares of a member where a debt was due from that member. The alteration was challenged. Lindley MR said as follows:

Wide, however, as the language of s 50 is (now section 21 of the CA 2006) the power conferred by it must, like all other powers, be exercised subject to those general principles of law and equity which are applicable to all powers conferred on majorities and enabling them to bind minorities stock. It must be exercised not only in the manner required by the law, but also bona fide for the benefit of the company as a whole, and it must not be exceeded. These conditions are always implied and are seldom, if ever, expressed. But, if they are complied with, I can discover no grounds for judicially putting other restrictions on the power conferred by the section and those contained within it.

In the instant case the Court of Appeal held that the power had been exercised *bona fide*.

4.3

COMPANY FINANCE

The role and definition of the promoter

Although there is no statutory definition of a promoter, case law has developed as definition. In the case Twycross v Grant (1877) a promoter is defined as "one who undertakes to form a company with reference to a given project and to set it going, and who takes the necessary steps to accomplish that purpose." In Emma silver Mining Co v Grant (1879) Lord Lindley stated that the term had no very definite meaning. Whether or not a person is a promoter is a question of fact. Promoters are quite often a company's first directors. The importance of establishing whether a person is a promoter lies partly in locating liability for acts done on behalf of or in connection with the company to be formed, for example, for statements in prospectuses. Not yet being in existence, the company cannot be liable. Promoters are not necessarily partners with each other (Keith Spicer and Mansell (1970)). Mainly it rests in deciding whether a person owes promoters fiduciary duty to the company.

Liability of a promoter

A promoter may become liable to third parties for misrepresentation or perhaps as the partner of another promoter under agency principles in partnership law. The traditional area of liability to the company is for breach of the fiduciary duties he owes it during his time of promotion.

Equity will not allow the promoter to taking advantage of his privileged position in relation to the unborn company. He must make full disclosure to it, when formed, of his interest in any transaction and must not profit from his position without the company's free consent. Otherwise, he must account personally for profits made and hold on constructive trust any property received which came to him by virtue of being a promoter.

A promoter must disclose fully the extent and the nature of his interest and profit. The duty cannot be avoided by setting up a company with a board of directors which cannot, and does not "exercise an independent and intelligent judgment on the transaction" and disclosing merely to that board.

In Erlanger v New Sombrero (1878) a syndicate headed by Erlanger, a French banker, acquired for £55,000 a lease of an island in the West Indies with phosphate mining rights. Erlanger then arranged for the syndicate to set up a company and to appoint its first directors, who were in reality puppets. The lease was sold, through a first party nominee, to the new company for £110,000 and within days of the company being established, the sale and purchase were ratified by the directors. The full details were not disclosed to members of the public who became shareholders. After the initial phosphate shipments proved unsuccessful, the true circumstances were revealed and the shareholders replaced the board of directors. It was held that the sale of the lease should be rescinded, the lease to be returned to the syndicate, which had to repay the purchase price to the company. The directors should not contribute to disadvantaging the shareholders. Disclosure to the members would be effective if they acquiesced (Lagunas Nitrate v Lagunas Syndicate (1899) but not if an undue advantage over investors remained e.g. if the original members comprised or were otherwise under the influence of the promoters (Gluckstein v Barnes (1990).

Remedies

The company may be able to rescind contracts entered into consequent upon non-disclosure or misrepresentation by a promoter unless one of the bars to rescission has become operative i.e. affirmation (unless this amounts to ratification of breach of duty by way of fraud on the minority: Atwool v Merryweather (1867); lapse of time; intervening third party rights; inability to make restitutio in integrum; and the courts discretion to award damages in lieu of rescission (Misrepresentation Act 1967 s2 (2)).

Breach of fiduciary duty may result in liability to account and/or imposition of a constructive trust. But promoters should be able to retain expenses incurred in acquiring property in such cases (Bagnall v Carlton (1877)).

Remuneration and expenses

The promoter does his work and incurs expenses by the nature of his position, at a time before the company has become legally capable of acting. The company cannot therefore enter into a binding contract with him to pay him, nor can the company when formed validly ratify such an agreement made when it did not exist (retrospectively validate).

It cannot enter into a new contract after formation (except under seal) for the consideration he provides will be past.

The practical solution is for promoters to secure the insertion in the articles of a provision enabling the directors to pay promoter's expenses plus reasonable remuneration, which provision will be valid if full disclosure is made.

Pre–incorporation contracts

Similar difficulties arise with contracts purporting to be made between the company and third parties before incorporation. The company will not normally be bound by preliminary contracts. Nor will the promoter be liable for breach of implied warranty of authority if no implication can be made, the third party knowing the true facts. The company may be liable apart from contract, to pay a reasonable amount for benefits actually received, or for conversion, for refusing to permit the third party to retake goods delivered.

Rather than attempt to bind a company, a promoter might contract personally with a third party and forward benefits received to the company when formed, under a separate contract, subject to full disclosure. He might make the company liable on his original contract by assignment.

Under The Companies Act 2006 s 21:

"A contract that purports to be made by or on behalf of a company at a time when the company has not been formed, has effect, subject to any agreement to the contrary, as one made with the person purporting to act for the company or as an agent for it, and he is personally liable on the contract accordingly."

The company's agent will be personally liable whether he purports to act on behalf of the company or signs the contract in the company's name alone, and he may be personally liable as both parties know the company is about to be formed and is not yet at the stage of being formed (Phonogram v Lane (1981). However, a person carrying out the affairs of an existing company under a new name which has not yet been registered will not be personally liable. Such a company is not one which has not been formed (Oshkosh B'Gosh v Dan Marbel (1988).

Trading certificate

A public company initially registered as such cannot commence business until the registrar receives a declaration that the nominal value of the allotted share capital meets the authorised minimum and, satisfied that it is, issues a trading certificate, (Companies Act 2006). This provision can be avoided by registering as a private company and registering as a public one.

Rules relating to payment for shares

The following matters should be checked where shares are to be issued by a public or private company:

- Does the company have sufficient authorized share capital for the issue?

This may be checked by looking at the company's memorandum. If necessary, the authorized capital may be increased.

- Do the directors have authority to allot the shares? See s. 549 of the CA 2006. However, a private company may pass an elective resolution that s. 549 is not to apply to that company, since, normally, authority under s.551 of the CA 2006 can only last for a maximum period of five years, unless renewed.

- Do pre-emption rights apply? Section 561 of the CA 2006 makes statutory provision for pre-emption on second and subsequent issues of shares. This may be excluded by a private company in its constitution. It may be excluded by both private and public companies by special resolution.

The rules for payment for shares are based upon the Second EC Directive on company law. They are incorporated into the CA 2006. Section 582 (1) of the CA 2006 requires that shares should be paid up in money or money's worth. Section 582 (1) of the CA 2006 provides that a public company cannot accept an undertaking from a person to do work or perform services for shares.

Section 580 of the CA 2006 requires that shares cannot be issued at a discount. This applies to both public and private companies. There are, however, exceptions to this principle:

- Shares may be issued to underwriters at a discount of up to 10 per cent (s. 553 of the CA 2006)

- Shares may be issued in exchange for services that happen to be overvalued in a private company. Shares may not be issued in exchange for services in a public company.

- Shares may be issued in exchange for property which is overvalued in a private company. In a public company, there is a need for an independent expert valuation of the property concerned (s. 593 CA 2006).

In a public company shares must be paid up at least one quarter of their nominal value plus the whole of any premium (CA 2006 s 586)

191

A public company cannot issue shares in exchange for a non cash consideration which may be transferred more than five years from the date of allotment (s. 587 (1) CA 2006).

Where shares are issued at a premium (that is above their nominal value) in either a public or private company, the whole of the premium is placed in a share premium account. This is treated as if it were ordinary share capital for most purposes. It cannot be used to pay up a dividend. However, it may be used to pay up a bonus issue of shares (s. 610 CA 2006).

The supervision and control of investments

The Financial Services Act 1986, as amended by the Financial Services and Markets Act 2000, provides for a regime to protect investors. The Act provides statutory regulation and self-regulation by the market. Deposit taking businesses are regulated by the Banking Act 1987. The Financial Services Act, as amended, gives certain functions to the Secretary of State but also authorises that person to transfer such functions as felt appropriate to a designated agency. This has been done in the first place to the Securities and Investment Board (S.I.B.) a body formed and supported mainly by the financial services industry.

Those who carry on an investment business must be "authorised persons" of whom a register is kept (FSA 1986 s102) or "exempted persons". (FSA 1986 s3). Otherwise they commit an offence and all transactions are unenforceable.

Authorisation may be made by membership of a recognised professional body (FSA 1986 ss15-21) or by the Secretary of State (FSA 1986 s25). The commercial method is by membership of a recognised self-regulating organisation such as the Financial Intermediaries, Managers and Brokers Regulatory Association (FIMBRA).

Exempted persons include: The Bank of England, clearing houses, Recognised Investment Exchanges such as the Stock Exchange and listed market institutions.

Except in the case of SRO's the Secretary of State is empowered to issue statements of principle and codes of practice regarding the conduct and financial standing expected of person authorised to carry on investment business (FSA 1986 ss57-58) and to make rules regulating the conduct of investment business by authorised persons for indemnification against civil liability incurred by authorised persons and for establishing a fund to compensate investors unable to obtain satisfaction of claims from authorised persons (FSA 1986 s54) and regulations with respect to money held by authorised persons (FSA 1986 s55).

The conduct of investment business

Subject to certain exceptions, the issue by or approval of an authorised person is necessary for the issue of an investment advertisement, which is an advertisement inviting people to enter into an investment agreement (FSA 1986 ss57-58). An investment agreement is one involving dealing or advising on investments, though not involving employee share schemes, sales of shares in private companies carrying over 75 percent of voting rights or where the terms of the transaction are uniform for all such transactions in the investment (FSA 1986 ss44(9) 20791) Sched 1). It is an offence knowingly or recklessly to make a misleading statement and to induce another to enter into, decline or refrain from exercising rights under an investment agreement, and without reasonably believing that he would not be so, to be involved in conduct creating a false impression as to the markets regarding investments and inducing a person to deal or refrain from dealing in those investments (FSA 1986 s 47).

On the Secretary of States application, the court may issue an injunction to prevent contravention of these provisions and order restitution of benefits (FSA 1986 s61).

The Securities market

For securities listed, or to be listed on the Stock Exchange it is necessary to comply with the requirements of the Financial Services Act 1986 part 1V. It empowers the Council of the Stock Exchange to make rules for this purpose, (FSA 1986 s142-144) including provisions for rectification for non-compliance with the rules. These rules on Admission of Securities to Listing

(The Yellow Book) contain continuing disclosure requirements. Additionally to information required by the yellow book, the submitted listing particulars must contain such information as investors and their advisors would reasonably expect to make an informed assessment of the present and anticipated future rights and financial status of the securities (FSA 1986 ss146-148) and copies must be delivered to the registrar. Where listing particulars are to be published in connection with an application for listing, no other advertisement should be issued without the approval of the Stock Exchange (FSA 1896 s154).

A person acquiring relevant securities is entitled to be compensated by persons responsible for misleading particulars for loss suffered by reliance on the information unless they reasonably believed the statements or any detail were properly omitted (FSA 1986 ss150-152), but shareholders have no right to challenge cancellations of listing by judicial review (R v Stock Exchange ex p Else (1992).

Unlisted securities

Companies which are inadmissible to the Official Listed Market may apply for admission to the Alternative Investment Market (A.I.M.). Offers of unlisted securities are governed by FSA 1986 Part V (FSA 1986 s158).

A person may not be responsible for the issue of an advertisement offering securities to be admitted to an approved exchange (R.I.E.) without the approval of the exchange and the delivery to the Registrar (FSA 1986s 159) of a prospectus. Similarly, a prospectus must be registered if the person is responsible for the issue of an advertisement for securities which is a primary offer (i.e. one inviting the initial subscribing for or underwriting of securities) or a secondary offer (i.e. by a person who has acquired shares from a purchaser) though the Secretary of State can make an exemption in cases where the general public is unlikely to require the relevant information.

Prospectuses must contain information prescribed by rules made by the Secretary of State and must contain all such information as investors and their professional advisors would reasonably expect to make an informed assessment of the present and anticipated rights and financial status of the securities (FSA

1986 ss163 and 164). Advertisements may not be issued for securities in private companies.

The main statutory rules are enhanced by the Public Offers of Securities Regulations 1995, which implement the E.C. Prospective Directive. They regulate first timer public offers of unlisted securities, subject to a number of exceptions (e.g. for denominations of less than ECU's 40,000). Free prospectuses must be published.

Subsequent dealings

A subsequent purchaser of securities on a market governed by the above rules should be protected by the securities having to comply with the rules governing the market. In addition, the ordinary law will also provide protection.

Criminal penalties and civil liability

The Financial Services Act, as amended, imposes a criminal liability for contravention of certain provisions. In addition it is an offence fraudulently or recklessly to induce someone to deposit money with any person (Banking Act 1987 s35). Under the Theft Act 1968 s19 a company officer causing or contributing to publication of a statement knowing it to be false or misleading, with intent to deceive members or creditors, may be imprisoned.

Civil liability

Whether on a first issue of or a subsequent dealing with shares, a person relying on a false statement may have a remedy against the company or the individual responsible. The following rules also apply:

- A person subscribing for or purchasing shares on the basis of misrepresentation may rescind the contract. The remedy is subject to the usual bars and to the courts discretion to award damages in lieu.
- Damages for breach of contract are unlikely to be available against the company, mainly because of the rules governing the maintenance of

capital and equal rights of membership, but such damages might be claimed from a transferor of shares.

- A person intending to rely and actually relying on a false representation made knowingly or without belief in its truth or recklessly may sue for damages for deceit, but a purchaser of shares in the market cannot sue if the representation is made as an inducement only to original subscribers unless it is also meant to mislead subsequent purchasers or is reactivated by a later statement.

- A defendant issuing a prospectus may be liable for damages for negligence to a subsequent purchaser of the companies shares on the unlisted securities market if the defendant intended subsequent purchasers to rely on the prospectus.

- At least before liquidation begins, a person is now no longer debarred from obtaining compensation from a company simply by virtue of his status as a holder for applicant, or subscriber for, shares. The Financial Services Act 1986 entitles a person to receive compensation for loss caused by false listing particulars and prospectus without having to relinquish his membership.

- A person acquiring securities on the basis of a false statement in listing particulars or a prospectus may claim compensation from persons responsible subject to defences of reasonable belief, ignorance or disclaimer.

- Damages for breach of statutory duty might be recoverable for omission of statutorily required details from prospectuses and courts have a discretion to award compensation in criminal proceedings.

The raising and maintenance of capital

Companies can raise capital to finance activities in a number of ways. The deferral of payments, through the acquisition of items on hire purchase or lease terms is one way. For the raising of substantial sums a company will need to obtain loans at preferential rates and will, more often than not, issue debentures, a form of promise to pay at a fixed rate of interest. Debentures can be attractive, depending on interest rates and tax advantages. Debentures will be discussed in greater depth a little later.

Companies will issue shares to raise capital. This is another very common method of financing. Shares are split into different classes of preference share providing different returns and levels of security to appeal to different types of investor. The rights of any preference shareholder are limited to the terms of issue of the class of share allotted. A dividend may be paid following from which there is no entitlement to share in any further income. Shares may be redeemable (at any point) in which case the shareholder cannot vote at meetings. The class of share will determine the rights, obligations and ultimate gains of the shareholder.

Share capital can be nominal, in other words the amount of money the company's memorandum entitles the company to raise. This can comprise issued share capital and un-issued share capital. Paid up capital represents the money actually received from shares sold and uncalled capital the amount owed.

Reserve capital is uncalled capital which the company has resolved only to call up on liquidation (Companies Act 2006). Shares may be issued at a premium (for more than their nominal value) if so the extra value must be transferred to a share premium account. Profits undistributed as income are kept in a reserve fund.

The liability of members of limited companies is limited to the nominal value of their shares. The nominal value of a public company's share capital must not be less than the authorised minimum, currently £50,000 (Companies Act 2006). One quarter of the value of all issued shares of a public company plus any premiums must be paid up. Shares must not be issued at a discount although debentures may. A commission may be paid to underwriters. Shares may be allotted for money or moneys worth. If shares are allotted for moneys worth, the consideration for allotment must be valued by an expert, whose report must be made to the company and made available to the allotee. Capital cannot be returned to members by the company. In general a company cannot acquire its own shares, subject to some exceptions (CA 2006 s 658).

A company must not provide financial assistance to another to acquire its or its holding company's shares. There are unconditional exceptions to this principle in s 681 of the CA 2006:

a) a distribution of the company's assets by way of a dividend lawfully made, or a distribution in the course of a company's winding up;

b) an allotment of bonus shares;

c) a reduction of capital'

d) a redemption of shares;

e) anything done in pursuance of an order of the court sanctioning compromise or arrangement with members or creditors;

f) anything done under an arrangement made in pursuance of s 110 of the Insolvency Act 1986;

g) anything done under an arrangement made between a company and its creditors that is binding on the creditors by virtue of Part 1 of the Insolvency Act 1986.

There are further exceptions for public companies in s 682 of the CA 2006:

- Companies may reduce their capital by passing a special resolution to this effect and obtaining the consent of the court to the reduction (s 641 (1) of the CA 2006)

- If a public company suffers a serious loss of capital (net assets worth half or less of called up share capital) then a general meeting is required to be called to alert the shareholders within 28 days of discovering that the loss of capital has occurred. The meeting should take place within 56 days (s 656 of the CA 2006).

Dividends to shareholders

Under s 820 the rules of the CA 2006 (from 2008) apply to 'every description of a company's assets to its members, whether in cash or otherwise'.

Section 830 (2) of the CA 2006 provides that distributions can only be made out of accumulated, realized profits less accumulated realized losses.

Section 831 of the CA 2006 applies to public companies. It requires the public company to maintain the capital side of its account in addition to having available profits. Therefore, if the company's net assets are worth less than the subscribed share capital plus undistributable reserves at the end of the trading period, that shortfall must first be made good out of distributable profits before a dividend can be made.

If a dividend is wrongly paid, a member may be liable to repay it under s 847 of the CA 2006.

Directors who are responsible for unlawful distributions can be held liable for breach of duty. If the directors have relied on auditors in recommending a dividend, then the auditors may be liable.

Becoming a shareholder

A person can become a shareholder by subscribing to a company, as per its memorandum or having shares transferred to him by an existing shareholder. Companies must keep a register of the class and extent of the company's shareholdings. A share is an item of property and usually freely transferable. It gives the holder an interest in the company measured by a sum of money and entitling him to the rights contained in the articles of association.

The value of the shares is generally their market price although a large number whose votes confer more may have a greater value.

Shareholders would usually have equal rights but companies can issue various classes of shares depending on the articles of association. The nominal value of a share specifies the maximum liability of a member of a company.

A share in a public company must be paid up by at least 25 percent but the company can make calls on the holder up to its unpaid value.

The articles may give the company a lien over the share for calls on the holder up to the unpaid value. They often empower it to forfeit the share for unpaid calls. A lien is an equitable charge on the share. It becomes effective on a specified event. Thus a different equitable interest of which the company has interest overrides a lien for debts due from the member (which it could set off against dividends) if the member only becomes indebted after the interest arose.

199

Under the Companies Act 2006, a company must, within two months of the allotment of shares or debentures or within two months of the lodging of a transfer of such securities, complete certificates, unless it is otherwise provided in their original issue, or it is not entitled to a certificate by virtue of the Stock Transfer Act 1982 (governing transfer of securities through a computerised system), or the allotment is to or the lodging of transfer is with a Stock Exchange nominee, or it is excused under the Uncertificated Securities Regulations 1995.

Transfer and transmission of securities

Formal documentation is usually necessary for the transfer of shares. However, the Secretary of State has been authorised to provide by regulation for title to securities to be evidenced and transferred without a written instrument. Otherwise shares are freely transferable. Articles of association may restrict transfer in which case a refusal to register must be made within two months of its being lodged and must not be made in bad faith. The seller should transfer his share certificate to the buyer so that the company will readily consent to registering him as a member. If the seller only transfers part of his holding, he should deposit his share certificate with the stock exchange (if PLC) or the company, which will issue a certificate of transfer.

Fully paid registered securities may be transferred by a stock transfer form approved under the Stock Transfer Act 1963. For a transfer to be registered by the company, unless the transfer is exempted by the Stock Transfer Act 1982, an instrument of transfer must be delivered to the company by either the transferor or the transferee.

Insider dealing

In recent years in particular, there has been controversy over the use of confidential information affecting the values of securities which is taken into account by the person in possession of it in deciding whether to buy or sell shares so as to make a profit. Insider trading, the use of knowledge by people on the inside of companies is seen as commercially immoral. However, it is extremely difficult to prevent. The only real deterrent is to impose criminal sanctions and to increase the powers of the various regulatory bodies.

The Stock Exchange requires listed companies to adopt its Model Code for Securities Transactions for Directors and to secure compliance with it. The Code warns directors to avoid insider dealing and requires them to refrain from dealing within two months before announcement of the company's results and to notify the company of such dealings.

The common law position in relation to insider dealing is based on Percival v Wright (1902). Shareholders offered to sell shares to directors who knew their true value was greater because of an impending takeover bid, which information their confidential obligations to the company forbade them to disclose. For that reason it was decided that the shareholders could not rescind the contract. The directors had no general duty to the shareholders to disclose price sensitive information to them.

The Companies Act 2006 imposes a statuary prohibition by making it a criminal offence for a director to purchase an option to buy or sell quoted shares or debentures to a company in his group. This liability is extended to his wife and children unless they had no reason to believe he was a director. The Companies Act also enacts requirements for disclosure and publicity. A director must disclose to the company details concerning the acquisition or disposal of any beneficial interest to himself, his wife or children in the group. If the shares are quoted the company must pass the information on to the stock exchange which may publish it. Any shareholders knowingly acquiring or disposing of a notifiable interest in voting shares (5 percent) in a public company must notify the company, which must keep a register of such interests.

There is also some administrative control.. Under the CA 2006, the Secretary of State can appoint inspectors to investigate suspected breaches of the various areas of the Companies Act.

The Financial Services Act 1986, as amended

There are certain provisions of the Financial Services Act that may apply to insider dealing. A private investor or other person suffering a loss from breach of a relevant rule may sue for damages for breach of statutory duty under the Financial Services Act ss61-62A.

The Criminal Justice Act 1993 Part V

If an individual knowingly has information which is insider information then he commits an offence if:

- Where the acquisition or disposal occurs on a regulated market, or where he acts or relies on a professional intermediary, he deals price affected securities.
- He encourages another person to deal in such securities knowing or having reasonable cause to believe that the acquisition or disposal occurs on a regulated market, or that the person dealing acts as or relies on a professional intermediary.
- He discloses the information to another person other than in the proper performance of his employment, office or profession.

The offence is punishable by a fine and/or up to seven years imprisonment. The Act has other provisions which provide for further sanctions and defences.

Borrowing money

In addition to issuing shares a company can raise finance by borrowing money. This is usually done in the longer term by issuing debentures. A Company may create a debenture fund and issue certificates for particular parts of the fund. The rights of debenture holders are fixed by the contract governing the loan. This is incapable of being altered even if, along the way, the articles are altered. Any attempted alterations represent a breach of contract.

Charges

Any form of security interest (fixed or floating) other than an interest arising by operation of law, is for the purposes of the Companies Act 2006 (Registration of charges) known as a charge.

Fixed and floating charges

A company can create a fixed charge over part of its property for the amount of the loan. Where a fixed charge is inappropriate, i.e. over fluctuating assets a floating charge over the whole or part of the company's assets can be made. The value of the charge as security depends on the assets in the company's possession at the time.

A charge must be registered within 21 days of its creation or the acquisition of property subject to it. The company and any officer at fault may be fined for non-registration. The court has discretion to extend a registration period. The Companies Act 2006 lists the registrable charges, including those on land, goods, intangible moveable property, i.e. intellectual property, for securing issues of debentures and floating charges. Not every charge is registrable, this very much depends on the nature of the charge.

Effects of non-registration

Where a registrable charge created by the company is not registered, the security is void against an administrator or liquidator of the company and any person who for value acquires an interest in or right over property subject to the charge where the beginning of insolvency proceedings, or acquisition occurs after the charge's creation. Where the registered particulars are not complete or accurate the charge is void, unless a court orders otherwise.

A registered charge, in general, gives the chargee a prior right, according to its terms, over a subsequent charge and any previous unregistered charges. But a subsequent floating charge can be created over a particular part of the assets covered by a previous floating charge over the wider category. A later fixed charge will gain priority over a previous floating charge covering the assets in question. In either case this is because floating charges are created with knowledge of the possibility of subsequent dealings with assets.

Unregistered chargees may prove in a company's liquidation as unsecured creditors and rank in priority as such. Fixed chargees can simply enforce their security according to the terms of the charge. The rights of floating chargees are, however, postponed to those entitled to preferential payments on a winding up (s196).

A floating charge created within 12 months of the onset of insolvency (24 months if in favour of a person connected with the company) or between the presentation of a petition for and the consequent making of an administration order is, unless the charge is not connected with the company and the company was solvent immediately after its creation, void except to the amount of any consideration provided simultaneously with or subsequent to its creation, plus interest.

****

Ch.5

BUSINESS LAW-INTELLECTUAL PROPERTY

PATENTS

The meaning of 'patent'

A patent is a monopoly right. The product or process, which is being patented, must first satisfy the criteria of the Patents Act 1977, which are:

1) There must be an invention, which must be capable of being patented but not an 'as such' invention. Certain inventions are non-patentable. This arises out of the Patents Act 1977 s1 (2) and (3)) The statute does not provide a clear definition of invention but the Patents Act sets out a list of things that are considered to be inventions 'as such': general abstract entities, aesthetic and non-technical things are considered to be excluded. Discoveries, scientific theories and other things such as mathematical methods are not considered to be inventions 'as such'.

One of the most problematic areas to arise out of this definition of things that are not regarded as being true inventions is that of computer programs. Despite not being considered inventions under the PA 1977 it is the case that patents for software related inventions are indeed granted. Software patents are granted when a substantial technical contribution is made, as this is not considered to be a computer program as such. One of several approaches is taken when deciding whether there has been a technical contribution:

> i) The question should be asked whether technical means are used to produce a result or solve a problem

ii)   Does the invention produce a technical result

2) Novelty must be present in the product or process which distinguishes it from other products and processes (PA 1977 s.2)

3) An inventive step must be present, i.e. the product or process must be seen as containing an clear element of invention (PA 1977 s. 3)

4) The invention must be capable of industrial application, i.e. must be of a purpose which can be applied to some form of industry (PA 1977 s.4)

Other areas of enterprise are not patentable 'as such'. Mental acts, schemes, rules playing a game or business methods.

Mental acts. In Raytheon (1993) an apparatus and process was claimed for the identification of ships. This involved the digital composition of the silhouette of the unknown ship with silhouettes of known ships, held in a computer memory. The claim was held to be excluded as it was merely an automation of a method normally carried out by individuals, i.e. a mental act as such. Carrying out the method with a computer did not create a technical effect.

Schemes, rules or methods for playing a game. Innovations in this area do not really amount to a technical contribution.

Business methods. The courts in the UK have always taken a strict approach to the patentability of business methods. Inventions must make a technical contribution but that contribution must not be in an excluded thing (such as a business method) and it is also seen that advances in business methods are not technical. More recent European patent office developments indicate that a more relaxed approach may be adopted. Whilst process claims to business methods are not inventions, 'as such' product claims may be patentable.

The presentation of information

The Patents Act 1977 s.1 (2)(d) provides that means of presenting information are not inventions 'as such'.

Non-Patentable Inventions

In some cases, rare though they may be, the commercial exploitation of an invention may be contrary to public policy or morality. Such an invention is unpatentable. The European Patent Office in Harvard/Onco-mouse (1991) when considering the patentability of a mouse or other non-human mammal genetically engineered so as to be predisposed to develop cancer, suggested that this should be addressed as a balancing exercise. Here the suffering of the mouse and the possible environmental risks were felt to be outweighed by the utility of the invention to humans, hence the Onco-mouse was not immoral.

As public policy and morality objections proved particularly problematic in the field of biotechnology, Directive 09/44/EC on the legal protection of Biological Invention provides further guidance on what is not patentable:

1) The formation and development of the human body and mere discoveries of elements of the human body (this includes gene sequences) are not patentable. However, where a technical process is used to isolate or produce elements (including genes) from the human body, this may be patentable.

2) Processes for modifying human germ line genetic identity (i.e. genetic changes that can be passed to the next generation.

3) Human cloning processes.

4) Genetic engineering of animals which is likely to cause the animal to suffer without a substantial medical benefit, either to man or to animals.

5) Plant or animal varieties or biological processes for the production of such varieties are not patentable, but inventions concerning plants or animals may be patented where the invention is not confined to a particular variety.

The concept of novelty

As discussed earlier, an invention must be novel (Patents Act 1977 s.1(1)(a) In UK patent law the terms 'novelty' and 'anticipation' are used interchangeably.

An invention must be new in the sense that it must not previously have been made available to the public. The Patents Act 1977 s.2 (1) provides that an invention is novel where it does not form part of the state of the art. Anticipation is judged by asking 'is the invention part of the state of the art'? Novelty is assessed objectively. In order for an invention to be anticipated, the prior art must either contain an enabling disclosure (in the case of a product patent) or, for process patents, it must give clear and unmistakable directions to do what the applicant has invented.

A key case here is Lux Traffic Controls Ltd v Pike Signals Ltd (1993) concerning what use amounts to disclosure to the public.. It was claimed that a temporary traffic signal was not 'new' because it had bee made available to the public in a paper, by oral disclosure, and by the use of a prototype which had been tested in public in Somerset.

The main principle to emerge from the case was that a prior publication must contain clear and unmistaken directions to do what the patentee claims to have invented: a signpost will not suffice. Where prior use is concerned there is no need for a skilled person to actually examine the invention as long as they were free in law and equity to do so and if a skilled person had seen it they would have been able to understand what the inventive concept was.

State of the art

The Patents Act 1977 s.2 (2) defines the state of the art as comprising all matter made available to the public before the priority date of the invention, this being the date of the first patent application. It therefore comprises all knowledge, global, on the subject matter of the invention. This knowledge can be made available in any way, either written, orally, or by any other means before the priority date.

The state of the art includes matter included in earlier patent applications, including those patent applications that are not yet published. Everything in the state of the art is known as prior art. Novelty destroying prior art could include information that is part of common general knowledge as well as specific pieces of prior art.

In some circumstances, a known invention may still be patented where a new use for that invention can be found, for example first medical use (Patents Act 1977) which provides that the first medical use of a known compound is novel, providing that the medical application of the compound does not itself form part of the state of the art (s.2 (6). Also second medical use. In Europe a policy has developed of allowing second and subsequent uses of known compounds. Such claims are novel where the second or subsequent medical use does nor form part of the state of the art and provided the patent application takes a very narrow form known as a Swiss Form Claim i.e. the use of medicament X for treatment of disease Y. The UK courts have sanctioned the use of Swiss Form Claims, but second and subsequent medical uses will only be novel in the UK, where there is a new therapeutic application, discovering information about a medical use is sufficient.

The Inventive step

An invention that is patentable must involve an inventive step. An inventive step is present where an invention would not be obvious to a person skilled in the art. In patent law, the term's 'inventive step' and 'non-obviousness' are used interchangeably.

Inventive steps are assessed from the perspective of the person skilled in the art (PA 1977 s.3), the skilled man. This hypothetical person has certain attributes, he is the average person in the relevant art, possessing the relevant skills, knowledge and qualifications. The statutory test for inventive step is embodied in what is know as the 'windsurfer' test. This test follows the approach set out in Windsurfer v Tabur Marine (1983) as modified by PLG Research Ltd v Ardon International Ltd (1995). According to the Windsurfer test, to test obviousness the following should be asked:

1) What is the inventive step involved in the patent?
2) At the priority date, what was the state of the art relevant to that test?
3) How does the step differ from the state of the art?

4) Without hindsight, would the taking of the step be obvious to the person skilled in the art?

When attempting to obtain a patent, it is important to note that patents are territorial rights, not universal and therefore it is necessary to apply for patents in each jurisdiction for which protection is desired. For example, a UK patent may be obtained from the Intellectual Property Office. Although there is currently no 'European Patent' as such, a so called 'bundle' of patents, national patents, from states that are party to the European Patents Convention 1973 (EPC) may be obtained by a single patent application to the European Patent Office.

The employee inventor – ownership of patents

When a patent is applied for, the basic rules are that a patent must be granted to the following:

1) The inventor or joint inventors i.e. the actual devisor of the invention. (Patent Act 1977 s.7(2) (a)
2) The inventor(s) successors in title
3) The employer of an employee inventor.

Ownership of employee inventions

Inventors have the right to be mentioned as such but the Patent Act 1977 provides that where the inventors are employees their employer will own the invention if:

a) The invention was made in the course of the employee's normal duties or in the course of specially assigned duties, provided that he or she might reasonably be expected to carry out those duties.
b) Where the employee has a special obligation to further the interests of his employer's undertaking. This is related to the

210

duty of fidelity that the employer owes to his or her employer.

Where the invention belongs to the employer, statutory compensation of the employer inventor may be available (PA 1977 s.40) provided that the patent is of outstanding benefit to the employer, the invention is subject of a patent grant and that it is just that compensation should be awarded.

There is a very high ceiling for statutory compensation and there has never actually been a reported case where statutory compensation under the 1977 act has been awarded. This is because such disputes tend to be settled out of court.

Patent applications may fail or those that are granted may be withdrawn on the basis of what is known as 'sufficiency'. A patent application consists of a number of components, and the patent specification is a vital part in which the invention is described and defined, it is the source of all the information about the patent that reaches the public domain. The specification must disclose the invention in such a way that the invention could be performed by the person skilled in the art. In other words, the application must contain an enabling disclosure.

The patent claim itself determines the scope of the monopoly granted to a patent proprietor. Claims must be clear and concise, be supported by the description and relate to a single inventive concept (PA 1977 s.14 (5).

Infringement of a patent

Certain activities carried out in the United Kingdom without permission of the patent holder constitute infringement (Section 60(1) and (2) of the Patents Act 1977:

1) Primary infringement. This falls into three categories:

 i) where a product patent is at issue, making, disposing of, using, importing or keeping the patented product (or disposal or otherwise)

ii)   where a process patent is at issue, use of the process with actual or constructive knowledge that non-consensual use constitutes infringement

iii)   The use, offer to dispose of, importation or keeping for disposal or otherwise of a product directly obtained from a patented process.

2) Contributory infringement. The supply or offer to supply any of the means that relate to an essential element of the invention, for putting the invention into effect may constitute infringement. This will only be the case where there is actual or constructive knowledge that those means are suitable (and are intended) for putting the invention into effect in the UK.

Exceptions to infringement

There are a number of exceptions to patent infringement set out in the Patent Act 1977 s.60 (5)(a)-(i) the main ones being:

- Private and non-commercial use
- Experimental use

The courts have considered whether repairs to patented products constitutes infringement. The position is quite clear, genuine repair of a patented product that has been sold for use does not constitute infringement. Anyone who wishes to attack a patent by claiming for revocation can do so on the grounds that the patent is not a patentable invention 'as such' or the invention is contrary to public policy or morality, the person granted the patent is not the person entitled to the patent, the patent specification does not amount to an enabling disclosure or there has been an impermissible amendment to the patent (PA 1977 s.72).

****

5.2

TRADE MARKS

Definition of a trademark and historical background

A Trademark is a symbol or a sign placed on, or used in relation to, one trader's goods or services to distinguish them from similar goods or services supplied by other traders. Section 1 of the Trade Marks Act 1994, which is the main legislation covering trade marks, defines a trade mark as any sign capable of being represented graphically which distinguishes the goods or services of one business from those of another.

International Provisions

There are a number of international conventions and arrangements that give some international recognition to national trademarks. These are the Paris Convention, The Madrid Arrangement and the Protocol to the Madrid arrangement (Madrid Protocol). There is also a Community Trademarks System that creates a trademark that gives rights throughout the European Community and which will be referred to below.

Trademark law

As seen, in the UK, trademarks are governed by the 1994 Trademarks Act. An application for a national trademark may be made to the Intellectual Property Office (see next chapter). Community Trademarks (CTM), a trade mark that is valid in the entire EU, may be obtained from the CTM Office, The Office for Harmonisation in the Internal market (Trademarks and Designs) (OHIM). Not all marks are capable of being registered as trademarks. Objections to the registration of a mark may be raised, either by the IPO during examination of the mark or by third parties during any opposition actions or proceedings. The grounds for refusing registration are divided into two categories:

a) Absolute grounds for refusal (TMA 1994 s.3 and 4) which are concerned with objections based on the mark itself.
b) Relative grounds for refusal (TMA 1994 s.5) these being concerned with a conflict and third party rights.

Classification of a trade mark

The Nice Agreement for the International Classification of Goods and Services provides that there are thirty-four classes of goods and eight classes of services. Any application for registration must stipulate which classes, or sub-classes, in which registration is sought. Multi-class applications are possible and it would, in theory, be possible to register a mark in respect of all forty two classes. However, this is very unlikely as applicants must have a bona fide intent to use the marks for the prescribed goods and services (TMA 1994 ss.3 (6) and 32 (3)).

Limited registration for retail service marks is also now possible in class 35. This change follows OHIM's decision in Giacomelli Sports Spa (1999).

Definition of a trade mark

The 1994 Trademarks Act s.1(1) provides that a trade mark is a sign capable of being represented graphically, capable of distinguishing goods or services of one undertaking, from those of another undertaking. There are a number of elements in the definition:

a) A 'sign'. The concept of a sign in UK trademark law is very broad indeed. Although there is no clear definition, signs provided in the UK include works, designs and shapes and also more unconventional marks such as sounds and smells. A sign can be regarded as anything that conveys information (Phillips v Remington (1998) See below.

b) *Graphic representation.* Signs must be represented graphically, i.e. be represented in such a way that third parties may determine and understand what the sign is,. This requirement is normally satisfied by including an image of the mark in the trade mark application. However, it has been suggested that provision of an image is not absolutely necessary provided that third parties can clearly identify the mark from the description (Swizzels Matlow Ltds Application (1999). It may be difficult to graphically represent unconventional marks, but practice dictates for example that sound marks are represented by music notation and that for shape marks it is best to submit line drawings or photographs. Applications for colour marks will usually include a representation of the colour and so on.

c) *Capable of distinguishing.* Signs must be capable of distinguishing goods or services of one undertaking from another undertaking. Any sign that has the capacity to distinguish will satisfy this requirement.

Marks devoid of distinctive character

TMA 1994 s.3 (1)(b) prevents the registration of marks that are not, prima facie, distinctive. An example might include a surname common in the UK. In British Sugar v James Robertson (TREAT) 1996, it was said that a mark is devoid of distinctive character where the sign cannot distinguish the applicants goods or services without the public being first educated that it is a trademark. The mark at issue in this case, TREAT, for a syrup for pouring on ice cream and desserts, was therefore devoid of distinctive character. Such marks may, nevertheless, benefit from the TMA 1994 s.3 (1)(b) proviso. Therefore trademarks will only fail where they are not distinctive by nature and have not become distinctive by nurture.

Signs that are exclusively descriptive

For a sign to be open to objection under TMA 1994 s.3 (1)(c) the trademark must consist exclusively of a sign which may be used in trade to describe characteristics of the goods or services. The sub-categories of TMA 1994 s.3 (1)(c) are:

1) Kind. Terms indicating kind or type that should be free for all traders to use, e.g. PERSONAL for computers, are not normally registrable.
2) Quality. Laudatory words, e.g. PERFECTION, are not usually registrable.
3) Quantity. The Trade Marks Registry gives the example that 454 would not be registrable for butter, as butter is frequently sold for domestic consumption in 454g (1lb) packs. Where numerical marks are not descriptive or otherwise objectionable, they may be registered.
4) Intended purpose. Generally, words referring to the purpose of goods or services are not registrable.
5) Value. Signs pertaining to the value of goods or services are not normally registrable, e.g. BUY ONE GET TWO FREE.
6) Geographical origin. Geographical names are not usually registrable unless used in specific circumstances.
7) Time of production of goods or the rendering of services. Typically, marks such as SAME DAY DELIVERY for courier services or AUTUMN 2004 for haute couture would not be registrable.
8) Other characteristics of goods and services. For example, a representation of the good or service would not usually be registrable.

Marks falling into any of these categories may still be registrable if they have become distinctive upon use.

Signs that are exclusively generic

TMA 1994 s.3(1)(d) prohibits the registration of signs or indications that have become customary in the current language or in the bone fide and established practices of the trade. An example can be found in JERYL LYNN Trademark (1999) where an application for JERYL LYNN for vaccines was refused as the mark described a strain of vaccine and was not distinctive of the applicant.

Shapes that cannot be registered

Traditionally in the UK, shapes were not registerable. One case highlighting this was Coca-Cola's trademark application (1986).

However, the TMA 1994 makes it very clear that the shapes of goods and their packaging are now registrable (TMA 1994 s.1 (1)), but the TMA 1994 s.3 (2) excludes certain shapes from registration. This is an area of trademark law that has lacked clarity.

ECJ guidance on the registrability of shape marks has clarified matters somewhat. The UK Court of Appeal stayed proceedings in Phillips Electronics v Remington Consumer products (1999) to allow a preliminary reference to the ECJ in a number of issues, including questions specific to shape marks and this decision has implications for the interpretation of the TMA 1994 s.3 (2). In this case, Philips had been producing a three-headed rotary shaver for a considerable time (the Philishave). When Remington produced a rotary shaver of a similar design Philips sued for infringement of a mark which was the face of the three headed shaver. The TMA 1994 provides that the following shapes are not registrable:

1) Where the shape results from the nature of the goods themselves. Inherent shapes therefore cannot be registered. In the Philips case, The Court of Appeal considered that there would be no objection to Philips three headed shaver shape on this ground as electronic shavers can take other forms.

2) Where the shape of the goods is necessary to achieve a technical result (TMA 1994 s.3 (2)(b). Functional shapes are therefore not registrable. In Philips 1999 case it was considered that the shaver shape was necessary to achieve a technical result, but the ECJ was, nevertheless, asked to adjudicate in the matter, i.e. on the correct approach to functional shapes. They concurred in the matter. They also confirmed that the fact that there may be more than one shape that could achieve the same result is not relevant. Consequently, it appears that only shapes with specifically non-functional aspects are registrable.

3) Where the shapes gives substantial value to the goods. In Philips (1999) the Court of Appeal suggested that a valuable shape in this context can be identified where the shape itself adds substantial value, e.g. the shape adds value via eye appeal or functional effectiveness. In contrast, shapes that are

valuable because they are 'good trademarks' would not fall foul of the TMA 1994.

Marks likely to give offence or deceive

A mark will not be registered if it is contrary to public policy or accepted principles of morality (TMA 1994 s.3 (3)(a) or is of such a nature that it is likely to deceive the public. For example, as to the nature, quality or origin of the goods or services.

Relatively few marks are deemed to be contrary to public policy or morality. Morality should be considered in the context of current thinking and only where a substantial number of persons would be offended should registration be refused.. For example, in BOCM's application, (EUROLAMB) (1997) EUROLAMB was considered to be deceptive if used in relation to non-sheep meat (when used in relation to sheep meat it was descriptive). It is very clear that the test of deception is deceptive and actual evidence of deception must be provided.

Marks prohibited by UK or EC law

The registration of marks whose use would be illegal under UK or Community law is precluded by TMA 1994 s.3(1)(d).

Protected emblems

TMA 1994 s.4 provides details of marks that are considered to fall into the category of specially protected emblems, e.g. marks with Royal connotations, and the Olympic symbol cannot be registered. Marks containing such emblems cannot be registered without consent.

Applications made in bad faith

The key statute here is Section 3(3)(a) and (b) and section 3(6) Trade Marks Act 1994, Art 3(1)(f) and (2)(d) Directive on the Legal Protection of Trade Marks:

(3) A trade mark shall not be registered if it is -

(a) contrary to public policy or accepted principles of morality, or
(b) of such a nature as to deceive the public
(6) A trade mark shall not be registered if or to the extent that the application is made in bad faith.

There is no requirement that a mark need be used prior to the application for registration, but the applicant must have a bona fide intention to use the mark and applications may be refused when they are made in bad faith. Therefore, so-called ghost applications should be caught by this section.

Relative grounds for refusal

Section 5(1) Trade Marks act 1994, Art 4(1)(a) Directive on the Legal Protection of Trade marks:

(1) A trade mark shall not be registered if it is identical with an earlier trade mark and the goods or services for which the trade mark is applied for are identical with the goods or services for which then earlier trade mark is protected.

The applicant must also overcome the relative grounds for refusing registration. These relate to conflict with earlier marks or earlier rights. The 'earlier mark' (TMA 1994 s.6) might be a trademark registered in the UK or under the Madrid Protocol. Alternatively it might be a CTM or a well-known mark (the latter are entitled to protection as per article 6 of the Paris Convention for the Protection of Industrial Property 1883).

There is no provision for honest concurrent use in the TMA 1994. As it has been made clear that a trade mark application must be refused, irrespective of honest concurrent use, if the registered proprietor objects, this provision is of limited value to the applicant. If the proprietor of the registered mark objects, honest concurrent use provides no defence.

Conflict with an earlier mark for identical goods or services

The TMA 1994 s.5 (1) only provides the narrowest relative ground for refusing registration: a mark identical to an earlier trademark and used for identical goods and services will not be registered. The requirement of 'identical goods and services' is sufficiently broad in scope to include cases where the applicants mark is identical to only some of the goods and services for which the earlier mark is registered, but to 'constitute an 'identical mark' a very high level of identity between the marks is required. One such case highlighting this is Origins Natural Resources v Origins Clothing (1995).

The registration of similar marks for the same or similar services is only prohibited where confusion on the part of the public is likely to arise (TMA 1994 s.5 (2). Specifically what is prohibited is the registration of:

1) Identical marks for similar goods or services or
2) Similar marks for identical/similar goods or services where, because of the identity or similarity, there is a likelihood of confusion on the part of the public, which includes the likelihood of association with the earlier trade mark.

What constitutes 'confusing similarity' has been considered at length by the ECJ (Sabel v Puma 1998) and Canon v Metro Goldwyn Meyer (1999). Confusion has to be appreciated globally taking into account all factors relevant to the case. These factors include:

- The recognition of the earlier trade mark on the market
- The association that can be made between the registered mark and the sign
- The degree of similarity between the mark and the sign and the goods and the services, the degree of similarity must be considered in deciding whether the similarity is sufficient so as to lead to a likelihood of confusion

It has also been made clear that 'likelihood of association' is not an alternative to 'likelihood of confusion" but serves to define its scope. This means that if the public merely makes an association between two trademarks, this would not in itself be sufficient for concluding that there would be a likelihood of confusion. There is no likelihood of confusion where the public would not believe that goods or services came from the same undertaking.

Conflict with a mark of repute

A mark that is identical or similar to an earlier mark will be refused registration in respect of dissimilar goods or services where the earlier mark is a mark of repute and the use of the later mark would, without the cause, take unfair advantage of or be detrimental to the reputed mark's distinctiveness or reputation. (TMA 1994 s5 (3).

A mark of repute is a mark with a reputation in the UK (for CTM applications it must have a reputation in the EU). In deciding as to whether a trade mark has a reputation, the ECJ has provided some guidance (General Motors Corp v Yplon) (2000). Repute would be judged with reference to the general public or to a specific section of the public, and the mark must be known to a significant portion of that public.

Relevant indicators of the public's knowledge of the mark include the extent and duration of the trade marks use, its market share and the extent to which it has been promoted.

In order for registration to be refused under s.5 (3) use of the applicants mark will have to take unfair advantage of or be detrimental to the reputed marks distinctiveness or reputation. In OASIS STORES LTD's application (EVEREADY) (1998) it was said that merely being reminded of an opponents mark did not itself amount to taking unfair advantage. The fact that the applicant did not benefit to any significant extent from their opponent's reputation and the wide divergence between the parties goods was relevant, s.5 (3) could not be intended to prevent the registration of any mark identical or similar to a mark of repute.

Conflict with earlier rights

TMA 1994 s.5 (4) provides that where a mark conflicts with earlier rights, including passing off, design rights and copyright the mark will not be registered.

Surrender, revocation, invalidity, acquiescence and rectification

Surrender. It is possible to surrender a trademark with respect to some or all of the goods or services for which it is registered. Marks may be revoked (removed from the registry on three grounds: non-use because the mark has become generic; or because the mark has become deceptive. A mark will be invalid if it breaches any of the absolute grounds for registration.

Where the proprietor of an earlier trade mark or other right is aware of the use of a mark subsequently registered in the UK and has, for a continuous period of five years, taken no action regarding that use the proprietor is said to have acquiesced. Where this is the case, the proprietor of the earlier mark or right cannot rely on his right in applying for a declaration of invalidity or in opposing the use of the later mark, unless it is being used in bad faith. Anyone with sufficient interest can apply to rectify an error or omission in the register. Such a rectification must not relate to matters that relate to the validity of the trademark.

Infringement

Section 10(1) Trade Marks Act 1994, Art 5 (1)(a) Directive on the Legal Protection of Trade Marks:

'A person infringes a registered trade mark if he uses in the course of trade a sign which is identical with the trade mark in relation to goods or services which are identical with those for which it is registered'.

The proprietor (and any exclusive licensee) has certain rights to a mark (TMA 1994 s.9 (1) which are infringed by certain forms of unauthorised use of the mark in the UK. These rights come into existence from the date of registration, which is the date of filing. All infringement acts require the mark to be used in the UK in the course of trade. What constitutes 'use' of a mark has been the subject matter of some debate and is discussed below.

Use of an identical sign for identical goods or services

Use, in the course of trade, of an identical sign, in respect of goods or services constitutes trademark infringement (TMA 1994 s.10 (1).

Use of an identical or similar sign on identical or similar goods or services

Use, in the course of trade, of an identical sign or similar goods or services (TMA 1994 s.10 (2) (a) or a similar sign on identical goods or services constitutes infringement where the public is likely to be confused as to the origin of goods or services or is likely to assume that there is an association with the registered mark.

Use of a mark similar to a mark of repute for dissimilar goods or services

Registered marks with a 'reputation' are infringed if an identical or similar mark is used for non-similar goods or services, where the use takes unfair advantage of or is detrimental to, the distinctive character or repute of the distinctive mark (TMA 1994 s.10 (3).

Contributory infringement

TMA 1994 s.10 (5) is known as the contributory infringement provision. This provision creates a form of secondary participation where a person who applies a trademark to certain materials has actual or constructive knowledge that the use of the mark is not authorised. This provision extends infringement down the supply chain, but printers, publishers, manufacturers or packaging etc. may avoid a s. 10 (5) liability in practice by inserting suitable contractual forms into their agreement with their clients.

Defences to infringement

a) Comparative advertising. Comparative advertising is allowed under certain circumstances as long as the use is not unfair or detrimental. One such case that highlights this is British Airways PLC v Ryanair Ltd (2001). British Airways had brought an action for infringement against Ryanair for the publication of two Ryanair advertisements comparing fares with

BA. The courts found that, in assessing as to whether a mark has been used in accordance with honest practice, the court should view the advertisement as a whole. Although misleading adverts cannot be honest, on the facts, whilst the advertisement at issue may have caused offence it was not dishonest and the price comparisons were not significantly unfair.

b) The use of another registered mark. The use of one registered mark, within the boundaries of the registration, does not infringe another registered mark.

c) Use of own name or address. A person using their own name or address does not infringe a registered mark, providing that the use accord with open honest practice.

d) Use of certain indications. The use of certain indications (e.g. the intended purpose of the gods or services or their geographical origin) will not constitute infringement where that use accords with appropriate honest practice.

e) The locality defence. Signs applicable to a certain locality whose use predates the registration of a mark may continue to be used in that locality.

f) Exhaustion. Trademark rights are exhausted once the proprietor has consented to the placing of goods bearing the mark on the market within the EEA. For example, once a brand owner consents to a consignment of their goods being marketed in France, trademark rights cannot be used to prevent these goods from being resold in the UK, unless there are legitimate reasons for this. Goods sold in this way are known as 'grey imports' or parallel imports.

****

5.3

COPYRIGHT

Definition of copyright

Copyright is the right to prevent others copying or reproducing an individuals or other's work. *Copyright protects the expression of an idea and not the idea itself.* Only when an idea is committed to paper can it be protected. Others can be directly or indirectly stopped from copying the whole or a substantial part of a copyright work. However, others cannot be stopped from borrowing an idea or producing something very similar.

Copyright is a right that arises automatically upon the creation of a work that qualifies for copyright protection. This means that there is no registration certificate to prove ownership. To claim ownership the author will have to produce original and preferably dated evidence of the creation of the work and proof of authorship. The author will also need to show that he is a qualifying person and that the work was produced in a convention country.

To be a qualifying person (s.154 of the Copyright Designs and Patents Act 1988) the author must have been, at the material time, a British Citizen, subject or protected person, a British Dependant territories citizen, a British national (overseas) or a British Overseas Citizen or must have been resident or domiciled in a convention country at the material time, which is when the work was first published. If the author dies before publication the material time is before his death. A convention country is a country that is signatory to the Universal Copyright Convention or the Berne Copyright Convention, which includes most countries in the world.

The works that can qualify for protection are defined in S.1 of the 1988 Act. These are:

a) Original literary, dramatic, musical and artistic works
b) Sound recordings, films, broadcasts and cable programmes

c) Typographical arrangements of published editions

Copyright – subsistence of copyright

Copyright is a property right that subsists in certain works. It is a statutory right giving the copyright owner certain exclusive rights in relation to his or her work.

In the 1988 Copyright Designs and Patents act there are nine categories of copyright works:

'Authorial' 'Primary' or 'LDMA' works

1) Literary works
2) Dramatic works
3) Musical works
4) Artistic works

'Entrepreneurial' 'Secondary' or 'Derivative' works

5) Sound recordings
6) Films
7) Broadcasts
8) Cable programmes
9) Typographical arrangements of published editions (the typography right)

Copyright comes into existence, or subsists automatically where a qualifying person creates a work that is original and tangible (or fixed).

Qualification

Copyright will not subsist in a work unless:

a) It has been created by a qualifying person
b) It was first published in a qualifying country
c) In the case of literary, dramatic and musical works, the work must be fixed, that is reduced to a material form in writing or otherwise

Copyright works

The CDPA 1988 defines a literary work as being 'any work written, spoken or sung, other than a dramatic or musical work'. A novel or poem could equally fall into this category. Additionally, the concept of literary works extends to tables (e.g. a rail timetable) compilations such as directories and computer programmes. Databases are also regarded as literary works. In essence, any work that can be expressed in print, irrespective of quality, will be a literary work.

Dramatic works

The CDPA 1988 defines 'dramatic works' as including works of dance or mime. In the case Norowzian v Arks (1999) it was stated that these terms should be given their natural and ordinary meaning, the implication being that dramatic works are works of *action*. The courts also recognised in this case that films may be produced as dramatic works, either as dramatic works in themselves and/or as a recording of a dramatic work.

Musical works

A musical work is a work consisting solely of musical notes, any words or actions intended to be sung, spoken or recorded with the notes are excluded. Therefore, a melody is a musical works with the lyrics being literary.

Artistic works

A wide-ranging definition of artistic works is provided by the CDPA 1988 s.4. Works of architecture are included but focus is usually placed on the remaining artistic works. These fall into two categories:

a)   Works protected irrespective of their artistic merit:

      i)   Graphic works, i.e. paintings, drawings, diagrams, maps, charts, plans, engravings, etchings, lithographs, woodcuts or similar works

      ii)   Photographs

      iii)   Sculptures. The protection of functional objects, such as a cast is problematic. In one notable case in New Zealand

Wham-O manufacturing Co v Lincoln Industries Ltd (1985) a wooden model of a Frisbee was held to be a sculpture. The modern UK position is almost certainly more restrictive, as objects will not now be protected as sculptures where they are not made for the purpose of sculpture.

iv) Collages. Collages are artistic or functional visual arrangements produced by affixing two or more items together. Intrinsically ephemeral arrangements (for example the composition of a photograph) are not collages.

b) Artistic works required to be of a certain quality (CDPA 1988 s.4 (1) c i.e. works of artistic craftsmanship. Few works can meet the standard of artistic craftsmanship, as they must be both of artistic quality and the result of craftsmanship. These principles were further developed into a two-part test for artistic craftsmanship in Merlet v Mothercare (1986). First, did the creation of the work involve craftsmanship in the sense that skill and pride was invested in its manufacturer? Second, does the work have aesthetic appeal and did an artist create it?

Sound recordings

A sound recording is a reproducible recording of either:

1) Sounds where there is no underlying copyright work (e.g. birdsong)
2) A recording of the whole or any part of a literary, dramatic or musical work.

The format of recording is of no relevance.

Film

The CDPA 1988 s.5B (1) provides that a film is a reproducible recording of a moving image on any medium. It is the recording itself that is protected, rather than the subject matter that has been recorded, but it should be borne in mind that a film might also be protected as a dramatic work. Film soundtracks are taken to be part of the film itself.

Broadcasts

Copyright subsists in sounds and visual images that are broadcast CDPA 1988 s.6 (1), a broadcast being defined as a transmission by wireless telegraphy of visual images, sounds or other information. The definition of 'broadcast' therefore encompasses radio and television broadcasts and both terrestrial and satellite broadcasting.

Cable programmes

The transmission of an item that forms part of a cable programme will create separate works that are capable of protection as cable programmes CDPA 1988 s.7. A cable programme service is defined as a service consisting wholly or mainly in sending visual images, sounds or other information via a telecommunications system which may utilise wires or microwave transmission. Items sent via wireless telegraphy are specifically excluded as they are already protected as broadcasts. This means that as well as subscription channels a website on the internet may be a cable programme service.

The typography right

The CDPA 1988 s.8 affords protection to the typography, that is the layout, of published editions of literary, dramatic and musical works. The leading authority on typographical arrangement copyright is Newspaper Licensing Agency Ltd v Marks and Spencer Plc (2001).

Copyright works the ideas/expression dichotomy

There is no copyright in ideas. Copyright subsists in the tangible expression of ideas and not the ideas themselves. In America this is referred to as the ideas/expression dichotomy. This principle can be helpful but should not be taken too literally, as whilst it is clear that mere ideas cannot be protected by copyright the following points should be noted:

1) What might be termed 'highly developed ideas', for example an early draft of a textbook, would be protected by copyright, as are preparatory design material for computer programmes.
2) Copyright cannot be circumvented by selectively altering the expression of a copyright work in the process of reproducing it.

Originality

The CDPA 1988 s.1 requires that literary, dramatic, musical and artistic works be 'original'. The originality requirements only apply to LDMA works, there is no such requirement for secondary copyright works, although it is clear that no copyright will subsist in secondary copyright works that merely reproduce secondary works.

LDMA works must be original in the sense that they originate with the author. One such case that highlights this is University of London Press v University Tutorial Press (1916). This is a minimal qualitative requirement: original works need not be inventive or original and a wide range of works have been held to be original, from coupons for football pools (Ladbrokes v William Hill (1964) to a compilation of broadcasting programmes (Independent Television Publications Ltd and the BBC v Time Out Ltd (1984).

Expending skill and judgement in creating an LDMA work usually suffices to deem the work original. Mere copying cannot confer originality. Alternatively, the mere expenditure of effort or labour (the so-called 'sweat of the brow' test for originality) has sometimes been said to be sufficient to confer originality. But in practice some minimum element of originality is required. For example, in Crump v Smythson (1944) it was held that the generic nature of commonplace diary material left no room for judgement in selection and arrangement therefore the resultant works were not original. Originality has also been held to be more than 'competent draftsmanship' (Interlego v Tyon

1988). Commonly databases and computer programmes were the subject matter of sweat of the brow concerns.

Higher standards of originality: computer programs and databases

As a result of two European Directives, The Directive on the Legal Protection of Databases (Directive 96/9/EC) and the Computer Directive (Directive 91/250/EEC) both computer programmes and databases must be original in the sense that they are the author's own intellectual creation. This is a higher standard or originality than that of 'skills, labour and judgement'.

Some databases may not meet the standard of originality to be afforded copyright protection. In this case the database can be protected by virtue of the *sui generis* database right.

The Database Directive which was incorporated into UK law by Part 1 1 1 of the Copyright and Rights in databases regulations 1997 grant a property right in a database whether or not it qualifies for a copyright work. The definition of database includes:

' a collection of independent works, data or other materials arranged in a systematic or methodical way and individually accessible by electronic or other means'.

A database can also be recognised as a literary work and thus afforded copyright protection. For this the database must be original and the contents and arrangements of the database must be a result of the author's own intellectual creation. In any case, all databases are protected by the new database rights irrespective of whether they qualify for copyright protection or not. To qualify for database rights the data must have been assembled through substantial investment in obtaining, verifying and presenting the contents. One case that illustrates this is British Horseracing Board Ltd v William Hill Organisation (2001)).

The duration of the database rights is for 15 years from 1st January of the year following completion of its making, or the first making public of the database within the 15 year period from its making.

Originality and the *de minimis principle*

The question arises, does copyright exist in very short works. The case, Exxon Corporation v Exxon Ind (1982), where the invented word Exxon was denied copyright protection, is often cited to support the proposition that a de minimis principle applies in copyright law, i.e. that some things are too small to be deemed copyright works. However, the authority for this is not so clear.

Fixation and tangibility

As we have seen, copyright does not subsist in literary, dramatic or musical works until they are recorded in writing or otherwise. This pragmatic requirement is known as 'fixation'. Usually, such works will be fixed by the author, but fixation by a third party (with or without the authors permission is also possible. Other copyright works are not subject to the fixation requirement. This is usually unproblematic as films, sound recordings, broadcasts, cable programmes and typography are inherently tangible works.

Ownership of copyright and the employee

The rule is that the first owner of copyright in a work is the person who created the work, i.e. the author. A major exception to this rule is CDPA 1988 s.11 (2). Which provides that where a person creates an LDMA work in the course of employment the employer is the first owner of any copyright in the work subject to any agreement to the contrary. There are special provisions for Crown use, Parliamentary copyright and copyright for certain international organisations (CDPA 1988 s.11 (3).

Authorship, ownership and moral rights

The author is the person who creates the work. Identifying the author is usually a straightforward task. The following is the standard authorship position:

- Literary work. The writer
- Dramatic work. The writer
- Musical work. The composer

232

- Artistic work. The artist
- Computer generated LDMA works. The person operating the computer.
- Sound recordings. The producer.
- Films. The producer and principal director.
- Broadcasts. The broadcaster.
- Cable programmes. The cable program service provider.
- Typography right. The publisher.
- Any work where the identity of the author is unknown. A work of unknown authorship.

Joint authorship

Where more than one person is involved in the creation of a work, careful consideration is needed in determining individual contributions. A person who suggests a subject to a poet is not the author of the poem. Merely supplying ideas is insufficient for joint authorship; an integral role in the expression of ideas is required. Joint authorship arises where the efforts of the two authors is indistinguishable.

****

5.4

INFRINGEMENT OF COPYRIGHT

Section 16(1) and (2) Copyright, Designs and Patents Act 1988 states:

The owner of the copyright in a work has the exclusive right to copy, issue copies of the work, rent, lend, perform, show, play or communicate the work to the public or do any of the above in relation to an adaptation.

Copyright in a work is infringed by a person who without the licence of the copyright owner does, or authorises another to do, any of the acts restricted by copyright.

The owner of copyright has the exclusive right to do certain specified things with the work and the right to grant licences to others or to take action for infringement. The acts, which the owner can do in respect of the work, are copying, issuing copies, performing or showing the work or performing in public or broadcasting the work. An adaptation is also protected as a copyright work.

The restricted acts will only be seen as infringed if the infringement is in relation to the whole or a substantial part of the work. Many infringement cases do indeed involve the reproduction of a substantial part of a work as opposed to the whole. Even if a defendant has built on the part of the copyright infringement and created a new work infringement still exists. There is no general test and each case is different.

If part of the claimant's work is itself an infringement of someone else's copyright that part will be disregarded in any infringement action.

It is an infringement if one person authorises another to do an infringement act. A well known case illustrating this point is Moorhouse v University of New South Wales (1976), where photocopying machines were available in the university library for use by students and other library users.

One particular person made two copies of a story from the claimant's book. The decision hinged on whether or not it could be said that the university authorised students to copy literary works without licence and whether, in this case, the university authorised infringement. It was held that notices around the library and in guides were held not to be enough, as they did not provide clear or adequate warning.

Copying works

This applies to all types of copyright work. In relation to literary, artistic, dramatic and musical works this means reproduction in any form, whether mechanical or electronic. However, for example, to make a recipe from a recipe book is not seen as reproduction as the person reading is utilising information that the author wishes to share. Artistic works may be infringed by reproducing a two-dimensional work in three dimensions and vice versa (s.17. (3) Of the 1988 CDPA). In the case of architect's plans, it would be an infringement to copy a plan or by building the actual building in the plan. However, it would not be an infringement to make a graphic two-dimensional work (drawing or photo) of a building or of a sculpture, model for a building or work of artistic craftsmanship in a public place because s.62 of the Act specifically says so.

Copying films, broadcasts and cable programmes is said by the 1988 Act as to include photographing any image in the film, broadcast or programme. Copying a typographic arrangement of a published edition means making an exact copy of a published edition. For example sending a published edition to someone by fax is not seen as reproduction.

In relation to the idea/expression divide in relation to deciding what is protected by copyright, even where it is obvious that an idea has been copied it does not necessarily constitute infringement unless the form of expression of the idea has also been copied. Determining this can be difficult. In cases relating to infringement of computer programmes, the use of different computer languages makes it more difficult. One such case highlighting this is Ibcos Computers Ltd v Barclays Mercantile Highland Finance Ltd (1994). In this case, the defendant had loaded a copy of the claimants software without permission, this being copyright infringement. Copying was proved by the existence of marked and unexplained similarities between the claimants and the defendant's code. In this case, the judge set out the correct test of copyright infringement in a case of non-literal copying. The court confirmed that, under English copyright law, the test for infringement was:

a) Is there a work?
b) Is it original?
c) Has there been copying?
d) Was this of a substantial part?

This is a simple but effective test that clearly lays out the guidelines for copyright infringement.

All copyright works may be infringed by the issuing of copies to the public. Issuing means putting into circulation copies of a work not previously put into circulation. This means that once a copy of a copyright owners work has legitimately been put out into circulation in any country the owner cannot prevent subsequent circulation of that copy (whether by sale, loan or distribution). However, the copyright owner still has the right to prevent the making of other copies from that one legitimately circulated copy.

Performing and playing of copyright works in public are also acts of infringement if done without licence. It is also an infringement of a copyright work to broadcast it or to include it in a cable programme service.

Adaptation of works
This act of copyright infringement only relates to literary, dramatic and musical works. Adaptation means a translation of a literary or dramatic work, the conversion of a dramatic work into non-dramatic and vice versa and reproduction of a literary or dramatic work in a form whereby the work is conveyed by pictures suitable for inclusion in a book or periodical. Adaptation also relates to conversion of a computer programme from one computer language to another, unless this conversion happens incidentally as a result of running a programme.

However, if the programme was translated in the course of running it on a computer, the act of making a transient copy of the programme (in either language) in the computer's memory would constitute making a copy and would be an infringement if done without the copyright owner permission. As a result of the EC Software Directive, implemented into English law by ss.50 (a)-(c) of the 1988 Act, a lawful acquirer of software has an implied licence to copy to the extent necessary for lawful use of the software.

Remedies

The remedies available to a copyright owner, and also to a licensee, for copyright infringement are to bring a civil action for damages, injunction to deliver up and also a possible criminal prosecution by the local weights and measures authorities for one or more of the criminal offences under the act, or to prompt seizures and fines by Customs and Excise and/or trading standards office pursuant to specific provisions of the act, the Trade Descriptions Act 1968 and the Copyright (Customs) Regulations 1989.

In the case of infringement the claimant may wish to apply for an interlocutory injunction, because the continued reproduction of infringing articles pending a full hearing could put the copyright owner out of business or be prejudicial in some other way.

An exclusive copyright licensee will have the same rights of the copyright owner in respect of an infringement committed after a licensee has been granted. With the exception of an interlocutory injunction, which the exclusive licensee must bring alone all other actions by a licensee must be brought in conjunction with the copyright owner.

In proceedings relating to copyright infringement, there are a number of presumptions laid down by the 1988 Act (in ss27(4) 104, 105 and 106) that allow certain issues to be assumed and that shift the burden of proof to the other party.

Defences to Copyright infringement

There are a number of defences to infringement:

a) Challenge the existence of copyright or the claimant's ownership of copyright.
b) Deny the infringement.
c) Claim to have been entitled, because of permission granted to do the act in question or argue that it is within one of the statutory fair dealing exemptions or by claiming public interest or EC competition rights.

A claim of ignorance of the law will not work as a defence. Ignorance of subsistence of copyright will, however, have a bearing on any damages awarded. In the case of secondary infringement an element of knowledge is required for the infringement to be actionable in the first place. The infringement only occurs if the person knows that what he or she is dealing with is an infringing copyright work.

If the claimant does own copyright in the work that is allegedly infringed, and facts can be proved, the only defences remaining are:

1) that the defendant had permission from the copyright owner to make a copy.

Provided that the defendant in an infringement action can prove that permission was granted, either in writing, orally or, in certain cases, implied, then the claim of infringement will fail.

2) That the act was one of the permitted acts under the 1988 Act.
The 1988 Act contains statutory permissions, or exceptions, to the exclusive rights of the copyright owner. Many of these have come from the results of case decisions over the years that have acknowledged the need for fair exceptions. These permitted acts are categorised in the Act and comprise:

- Research and private study
- Criticism review and news reporting
- Incidental inclusion of copyright material
- Things done for instruction or examination

- Anthologies for educational use
- Playing, showing or performing in an educational establishment
- Recordings by educational establishments
- Reprographic copying by educational establishments
- Libraries and archives
- Public administration
- Lawful users of computer programs and databases
- Designs
- Typefaces
- Works in electronic form

All of the above are categorised in the Act and each case concerning these categories will be on its own merit.

3) That the exercise of the copyright owner's rights to prevent copying would amount to an anti-competitive practice under EC competition law.

4) That the exercise of the copyright owner's rights is against the public interest.

Each one of the above must be proven and each case will be judged on its own merit.

****

5.5

DESIGN LAW

Design

A design may be protected in a number of ways, in particular by the Community Design, (Registered Design and Unregistered Design) the UK Registered Design and the UK Unregistered Design Right.

Community Design

There are two forms of Community design, one subject to registration (RCD) and the other informal (UCD). The basic requirements are both the same, apart from the date at which novelty and individual character is tested.

A community design has a unitary character and has equal effect throughout the Community. It may only be registered, transferred, surrendered, declared invalid or its use prohibited in relation to the entire community.

The main legislation dealing with community design is Article 3 Community Design regulation OJ 2002 L341:

a) 'design' means the appearance of the whole or part of a product resulting from the features of, in particular, the lines, contours, colours, shape, texture and/or materials of the product itself and /or its ornamentation;

b) 'product means any industrial or handicraft item, including *inter alia* parts intended to be assembled into a complex product, packaging, get up, graphic, symbols and typographic typefaces but excluding computer programs:

c) 'complex product' means a product which is composed of multiple components which can be replaced, permitting disassembly and re-assembly of the product.

Article 4 (1) Community Design regulation

A design shall be protected by a community design to the extent that it is new and has individual character.

Novelty and Individual character

A design is new if no identical design (including a design with features which differ only in immaterial details) has been made available to the public. There is a proviso to this and that is a pre-existing design will be disregarded if it could not reasonably have become known in the normal course of business to the circles specialized in the sector concerned operating in the community.

A design has an individual character if the overall impression it produces on an informed user differs from the overall impression produced on such a user by any design which has been made available to the public.

A key case concerning novelty and individual character is that of Green Lane Products Ltd v PMS International Group Ltd (2008). In this case, a challenge to the validity of the claimant's Community design for spiky laundry balls was based on the defendant's similar shaped spiky balls used for massaging the human body.

It was established in this case that the prior art is not limited to the particular product for which the design was registered, as the scope of infringement is not limited to the product for which it was intended to apply the design. For example, the registration of a design intended for motor cars would protect also against its use for toys.

The 'informed user' is not the same as the average consumer of trade mark law. The informed user has experience of similar products and will be reasonably discriminatory and able to appreciate sufficient detail to decide whether or not the design under consideration creates a different overall impression. The degree of design freedom is taken into account.

A key case concerning individual character and design freedom is that of Pepsico Inc's design (No ICD000000172) OHIM.

The design in question was for a disk having annular rings or corrugations applied to a promotional item for games. There was a challenge to the validity of the design. The design was declared invalid.

The legal principle was that the informed consumer would be familiar with promotional items and would pay more attention to graphical elements rather than minor variations in shape. Furthermore, although there were some constraints to design freedom, these were to do with cost and safety, and, otherwise, there was ample design freedom. Thus, the informed user may focus on certain aspects of a design and design freedom should be looked at in the round and some constraints may be present without significantly reducing the overall design freedom.

Time periods for testing novelty and individual character

The time when a design has been made available to the public differs between the RCD and the UCD (Registered and Unregistered). The RCD relevant date is the date of filing the application, or earlier priority date if there is one. The UCD relevant date is the date the design itself is first made available to the public.

There is a 12-month period of grace for the RCD so, for example the designer may market products relating to that design during that period before filing the application to register.

"Under the bonnet' parts which are not seen during normal use of a complex product are not considered to be novel or have individual character.

Exclusions from Community Design

The below are exclusions from community design:

- Features dictated by technical function
- 'Must-fit' features (except in respect of modular systems which are protectable in principle)
- Designs contrary to public policy or morality

- "Must-match' spare parts used to restore the original appearance of a complex product.

Duration

Registered Community Designs – five years from the date of filing. It may then be renewed for further periods of five years up to a maximum of 25 years. Unregistered Community Designs-three years from the date the design was first made available to the public.

For the purpose of the unregistered design in determining the start of the three years, it is made available to the public when it is published, exhibited, used in trade or other wise disclosed in such a way that, in the normal course of the business, these events could have reasonably have become known to the circles specialized in the sector concerned in the community.

Protection and infringement of a community design

The scope of protection of a community design resembles the test for individual character in that it is a question of whether the alleged infringing design, from the perspective of the informed user, does not produce a different overall impression compared with the protected design. Design freedom is taken into consideration.

The main legislation concerning protection of community design is Article 10 Community Design Regulation OJ 2002 L341:

1) The scope of protection conferred by a community design shall include any design which does not produce on the informed user a different overall impression.

2) In assessing the scope of protection, the degree of freedom of the designer in developing his design shall be taken into consideration.

The registered community design gives the rightholder a monopoly right which is infringed by a person using it without the rightholders consent. Use, in particular, includes making, offering, putting on the market, importing, exporting or using a product in which the design is incorporated or applied, or stocking such a product for those purposes.

For the unregistered Community design, it is required that the use in question results from copying the protected design. This also applies during the period of deferred publication where the design is registered but publication has been deferred. An applicant to register a Community design can defer publication by up to 30 months from the filing date, hence delaying the payment of the publication fee.

A key case concerning infringement was that of Procter and Gamble Co v Reckitt Benckiser (UK) Ltd (2008) which was a case on the alleged infringement of a registered Community design applied to a spray container for air fresheners.

It was found in this case that a design did not have to be clearly different, it was sufficient if it differed in a way that the informed user was able to discriminate. An initial decision that there had been an infringement was reversed.

Limitations on the rights to a Community design

The rights to a Community design (registered or unregistered) do not extend to the following acts:

- Acts done privately and for non-commercial purposes.
- Acts done for experimental purposes
- Reproduction for citation or teaching in accordance with fair practices without unduly prejudicing the normal exploitation of the design, providing the source is mentioned.
- Acts in respect of the repair of ships or aircraft temporarily in the Community.

UK registered design

The UK registered design has been modified as a result of the EU Directive harmonising registered design law throughout the European Community. As a result, the main principles in the EU and UK are virtually identical.

245

The main legislation dealing with registered designs in the UK is section 24A (2) of the Registered Designs Act 1949 and Regulation 1A (2) Community Design regulations 2005/2339, as amended:

In an action for infringement (of a Community Design) all such relief by way of damages, injunctions, accounts or otherwise is available to him as is available in respect of the infringement of any other property right.

There is also a remedy for groundless threats of infringement proceedings which applies in respect of a community design (registered and unregistered. there is an equivalent remedy for the UK unregistered design right.

UK unregistered design right

The UK unregistered design right was introduced by the Copyright, Designs and Patents Act 1988 in an attempt to overcome the problems of protection of functional designs by means of copyright in drawings showing the designs, as highlighted in *British Leyland Motor Corp v Armstrong patents Co Ltd (1986).*

The main legislation Section 213(1), (2) and (4) Copyright, Designs and Patents Act 1988 states:

(1) Design right is a property right which subsists in accordance with this part in an original design.

(2) In this part, 'design' means the design of any aspect of the shape or configuration (whether internal or external) of the whole or part of an article.

(3) A design is not 'original' for the purposes of this part if it is commonplace in the design field in question at the time of its creation.

Exceptions to subsistence of UK unregistered design right

Sections 213 (3) Copyright, Designs and Patents act 1988 states:
(3) Design right does not subsist in -

(a) a method of principle of construction,
(b) features of shape or configuration of an article which -

(i) enable the article to be connected to, or placed in, around or against another article so that either article may perform its function, or

(ii) are dependant upon the appearance of another article of which the article is intended by the designer to form an integral part, or

(c) surface decoration.

The first exception, methods or principles of construction, is unlikely to be relevant in the majority of cases. then other exceptions are often referred to as the 'must fit' or 'must match' exceptions. Surface decoration is also excepted.

A key case in the area is that of Dyson Ltd v Qualtex (UK) Ltd (2006) which concerned various aspects of design right including the scope of the 'must fit' and 'must match' and surface decoration exclusions.

The facts of the case were that the defendant supplied duplicate spare parts (pattern parts) for the claimant's vacuum cleaners. The claimant sued on the basis of the unregistered design rights subsisting in the design of the parts of its vacuum cleaners.

The court found that the 'must fit' exclusion does not mean that the articles have to physically touch. A clearance between them, if it allows one article to perform its function, may be within the exclusion. the exclusion may apply where the two articles are designed sequentially one after the other.

For 'must match' exclusion it is the design dependency which is important. the more room there is for design freedom, the less likely the exception will apply. The reason for the surface decoration exclusion was because it was protected by copyright. Surface decoration could be applied to a two-dimensional article or three dimensional article or to a flat surface of a three dimensional article. Surface decoration was not limited to something applied to an existing article and it could come into existence with the surface itself. Surface decoration could be three dimensional such as beading applied to furniture. However, a feature having a function, such as ribbing on the handle of a vacuum cleaner, was unlikely to be surface decoration.

****

INDEX

Acceptance of an offer, 13
Action for an agreed sum, 69
Action for wrongful dismissal, 149
Adams v Lindsell (1818), 14
Adaptation of works, 237
Additional Paternity Leave
    Regulations 2010, 138
Adoption leave, 139
Adoption leave and pay, 139
Advertisements, 11
Age discrimination, 164
Agreement, 95
Agreement by deed, 31
Alternative Investment Market
    (A.I.M.), 194
Alternative Investment Market
    (A.I.M.)., 194
Amalgamated Investment and
    Property Co Ltd v John Walker
    and sons Ltd (1977), 39
Annual General Meeting, 170
Apportionment, 94
Apprentices, 123
Armhouse Lee Ltd v Chappell
    (1996), 51
Articles of association, 183, 200
Artistic works, 226, 227, 228, 236
Association of British Travel
    Agents, 11
Auction sales, 17

Balfour v Balfour (1919), 19
Banking Act 1987, 192, 195
Becoming a shareholder, 199
Bilateral contracts, 8, 11
Borrowing money, 202
Bowerman v Association of British
    Travel Agents Ltd (1996), 11
Breach of a condition, 64
Breach of duty, 82
Breach of legislation, 46
Breach of statutory duty, 110
Breach of terms concerning time,
    61
British Road Services v Crutchley
    (Arthur V) Ltd (1968), 13
Broadcasts, 226, 229, 233

Cable programmes, 226, 229, 233
Car and Universal Finance Co Ltd
    v Caldwell (1965), 37
Carelessness, 74
Carlill v Carbolic Smokeball
    (1893), 8
Causation, 3, 67, 87, 93, 112
Certainty of contract, 18
Change of name, 182
Characteristics of the defendant,
    84
Charges, 203
Chartered corporations, 22
Children, 93, 106

Civil Evidence Act 1968, 85
Classification of a trade mark, 214
Collateral agreements, 34
Commercial agreements, 19
Common duty of care, 105
Common law negligence, 116
Common mistake, 39, 40
Communicating acceptance of an
offer, 14
Communication of offers, 11
Community Design, 241, 242, 243,
244, 246
Community Interest Companies,
171
Companies Act 2006, 168, 169,
172, 173, 177, 179, 180, 181,
182, 183, 189, 190, 197, 200,
201, 203
Companies House, 167, 182
Company Directors
Disqualification Act 1986, 173
Company limited by guarantee,
168
Company names, 181
Competition law, 50
Conciliation, 157
Conflict with a mark of repute,
221
Conflict with earlier rights, 222
Confusion, 220
Consideration, 3, 7, 25, 26, 27, 65
Construction of express terms in
contracts, 35

Constructive dismissal, 146
Consumer Credit Act 1974), 7, 22
Consumer Protection Act 1987,
113
Contracts against public policy, 51
Contracts in restraint of trade, 47
Contracts prejudicial to public
safety, 51
Contracts which must be
evidenced in writing, 23
Contracts which must be in
writing, 22
Contracts which must be made by
deed, 22
Contributory infringement, 212,
223
Contributory negligence, 77, 93
Copying works, 236
Copyright, 225, 226, 227, 229, 230,
231, 235, 238, 246
Copyright (Customs) Regulations
1989, 238
Corporate personality, 172
Corporation tax, 167
Corporations, 21
County Ltd v Girozentrale
Securities (1996), 67
Covenants in restraint of trade,
122
Cross-purpose mistake, 39
Cundy V Lindsey (1878), 41

Damages against employee, 149

Dangerous goods, 113
Databases, 227, 231
Davis Contractors Co Ltd v
  Fareham UDC (1956), 62
Death of either party to the
  contract, 61
Debentures, 196
Defective good, 79
Defective property, 79
Definition of a trade mark, 214
Design, 2, 241, 244, 246
Designs, 213, 225, 226, 240
Disability Discrimination Act
  1995, 164
Disability Discrimination Act
  1996, 159
Dismissal, 145, 152, 155, 161
Dismissal for trade union reasons,
  155
Dismissal with notice, 145
Dismissals Procedure, 147
Dividends, 198
Dividends to shareholders, 198
Doctor, 73
Domestic and social agreements,
  19
Dramatic works, 226, 227
Dunlop Pneumatic Tyre Co Ltd v
  New Garage and Motor Co Ltd
  (1915), 71
Duress, 3, 53
Duties of the employer, 122
Duty of care, 73

Economic duress, 53, 54
Economic loss, 75
Employee inventions, 210
Employee inventor, 210
Employer, 3, 73, 99, 100
Employer's Liability (Defective
  Equipment) Act 1969, 100
Employers Liability, 99
Employers Liability (Compulsory
  Insurance) Act 1969., 99
Employment Appeal Tribunal, 157
Equal Pay, 159, 160, 161, 162
Equal Pay (amendment)
  Regulations 1983, 159
Equal Pay Act 1970, 159, 160
Equality Act 2010, 126, 133, 159,
  160, 163, 164
Equitable remedies, 69
Errington v Errington (1952), 13
Establishing Authorship, 232
Ex Turpi Causa, 96
Exceptions to infringement, 212
Executory consideration, 26
Existing contractual duty to a
  third party, 29
Existing public duty, 28
Extent of damage, 90
Extraordinary General Meeting,
  169

Film, 229
Films, 226, 233

Financial Intermediaries,
Managers and Brokers
Regulatory Association
(FIMBRA), 192
Financial loss, 76
Financial Services Act 1986, 193
Financial Services and Markets Act
2000, 192
Fixed and floating charges, 203
Fixed charge, 203
Flexible working, 141
Floating, 203
Formalities, 22, 65
Frost v Knight (1872), 64
Frustration of contract, 61

Gaming Act 1845, 50
Gibson v Manchester City
Council (1979), 9
Glasbrook Brothers v Glamorgan
County Council (1925), 28
Group structures, 174

Hadley v Baxendale (1854), 68
Hart v O'Connor (1985), 21
Hartley v Ponsonby (1857), 28
Harvey v Facey (1893), 17
Henderson v Arthur (1907), 34
Holiday pay, 132
Hughes v Metropolitan Railways
Co (1875), 30
Human cloning processes, 207
Hyde v Wrench (1840), 12

Ignorance of the offer, 15
Illegal contract, 52
Illegal mode of performance, 45
Implied terms, 34, 35
Impossible to fulfill contract, 61
Independent contractors, 107, 110
Inequality of bargaining power, 56
Infringement, 4, 211, 222, 235
Infringement of a patent, 211
Infringement of Copyright, 4, 235
Injunction, 150
Injunctions, 70
Insider dealing, 200
Insolvency Act 1986, 170, 173, 198
Intention to create legal relations,
18
Intervening causes, 91
Intervening natural force, 92
Invitation to treat, 9

Job applications and
discrimination, 165
Joint authorship, 233

Knowledge of the risk, 95

Landlord and Tenant Act 1954,
174
Law of Property (Miscellaneous
Provisions) Act 1989, 31
Law of Property Act 1925, 22
Law of Property Act 1969, 173
Levy v Yates (1838), 45

Liability of a promoter, 187
Limited Liability Partnerships, 170
Limited Liability Partnerships Act 2000, 170
Literary works, 226
Liverpool Council v Irwin (1977), 36
Lloyds Bank v Bundy (1974), 55
Loss of expectation, 68

Madrid Arrangement, 213
Madrid Protocol, 213, 219
Manufacturer, 73, 117
Marks devoid of distinctive character, 215
Marks prohibited by UK or EC law, 218
Maternity, 133, 135, 136, 137
Maternity and Parental Leave Regulations 1999, 137
Maternity leave, 133
Medical negligence, 88
Memorandum of association, 177
Mental acts, 206
Mental incapacity, 20
Method of performance impossible, 61
Misrepresentation, 36, 38, 77, 188
Misrepresentation Act 1967, 77, 188
Mistake as to title, 41
Mistake over the terms of the contract, 42

Mistaken identity, 41
Mitigation, 60, 68
Musical works, 226, 227

National Minimum Wage, 123
National Minimum Wage Act (NMW) 1998, 123
National security, 156
Negligence, 3, 67, 73, 82, 87, 93, 96, 107, 175
Negligent acts, 78
Neighbour principle, 74
Nice Agreement, 214
Night work, 131
Non-Patentable Inventions, 207
Non-specific tenders, 17
North Ocean Shipping Co v Hyundai Construction Co (The Atlantic Baron) (1979), 53
Novelty, 206, 208, 242

Objects clauses, 178
Occupiers Liability, 102, 103, 104, 107, 108
Offer and acceptance, 8
Offers of sale, 10
Omissions, 82
Oral statements, 33
Originality, 230, 231, 232

Parental leave, 137
Paris Convention, 213, 219
Part Time Workers, 142, 143

Partially written agreements, 34
Partnership, 167, 170
Partnerships, 167
Partridge v Crittendon (1968), 11
Part-Time Workers (Prevention of
Less Favourable Treatment)
Regulations 2000, 142
Patent, 205, 207, 210, 211, 212
Patents, 122, 205, 207, 208, 209,
210, 211, 225, 226, 235, 246
Paternity leave, 137, 138
Performance made pointless, 62
Performance of an existing duty,
27
Performance under contract, 59
Personal Protective Equipment at
Work Regulations 1992, 100
Pharmaceutical Society of Great
Britain v Boots Cash Chemists
(Southern) Limited 1953, 10
Police, 96, 101
Pre-hearing Assessments, 157
Pre–incorporation contracts, 189
Prevention of performance by one
party, 60
Primary infringement, 211
Promisee, 25
Promisor, 25
Promissory estoppel, 29, 30
Promoters, 187
Proof of negligence and damage,
118

Property management companies,
171
Protected emblems, 218
Provision and Use of Work
Equipment Regulations 1992,
100
Psychiatric illness, 80
Public companies, 167
Public Limited Company, 167
Public Offers of Securities
Regulations 1995, 195
Pure economic loss, 76, 118

Race Relations Act 1976, 159, 163
Re Moore and Co Ltd and
Landaur and Co (1921), 60
Reasons for dismissal, 154
Rectification, 34, 44
Redundancy, 154
References, 155
Registered companies, 21
Registered Designs Act 1949, 246
Reliance loss, 69
Remedies, 3, 65, 67, 71
Remedies agreed by the parties, 71
Remedies for breach of contract,
65
Remedy for breach of contracts, 67
Remoteness, 3, 67, 68, 87, 88
Remuneration, 160, 189
Repudiation, 64
Rescuers, 94
Restitution, 69

Retirement and age
discrimination, 165
Roscords v Thomas (1842), 26

Safe plant and equipment, 100
Sale of Goods act 1979, 18
Sale of land, 17
Scammell v Ouston (1941), 18
Scotson v Pegg (1861), 29
Securities market, 193
Severable contracts, 60
Sex Discrimination Act 1975, 159,
160
Sex Discrimination Act 1986, 126,
159, 161
Sexual Orientation, 159, 163
Shirlaw v Southern Foundries
(1926), 35
Shock victims, 80
Social agreements, 19
Solicitor, 73
Sound recordings, 225, 226, 228,
233
 recial standards of care, 83
cific performance, 69, 70, 150
cific tenders, 16
of the art, 208
ory companies, 21
ry intervention, 179
y Maternity Pay, 135
lyrick (1809), 28
nsfer Act 1982, 200
lity, 100

Substantial performance, 60
Summary dismissal, 146
Suspension, 151

Taylor v Caldwell (1863), 61
Tenders, 16
Termination by agreement, 148
Termination by frustration, 148
Terms implied into contract by
statute, 18
Terms of contracts, 33
the bill of exchange. Under s27 of
the, 26
The capacity to enter into a
contract, 20
The Criminal Justice Act 1993,
202
The effect of an illegal contract, 51
The Financial Services Act 1986,
192, 196, 201
The inventive step, 209
The Maternity and Parental Leave
Regulations 1999, 137
The Nice Agreement for the
International Classification of
Goods and Services, 214
The typography right, 229
Third party, 77, 78
Time of frustrating event, 63
Time off for ante-natal care, 135
Torts (Interference With Goods)
Act 1977, 93
Tortuous negligence, 92

Trade Descriptions Act 1968, 238
Trade Marks, 4, 213, 216, 218, 219, 222
Trade Marks Act 1994, 213
Trade Union and Labour
    Relations (Consolidation) Act
    1992, 150, 155
Trademark, 213, 216, 224
Trademarks, 213, 214
Trades Mark Act 1994, 182
Trading certificate, 190
Transfer and transmission of
    securities, 200
Trespassers, 107, 109

UK registered design, 245
UK Unregistered Design Right, 241
Undue influence, 54
Unfair Contract Terms Act 1977, 38, 77, 105, 107, 109
Unfair dismissal, 165
Unfair Dismissal, 151

Unilateral contract, 8
Unilateral contracts, 8
Unlisted securities, 194

Vicarious liability, 102
Violenti Non Fit Injuria, 94
Visitors, 104, 108
Voluntary work, 124

Wagering contracts, 50
Waiver, 29, 147
Walker v Boyle (1982), 38
Working Time Regulations, 127
Working Time Rights, 128
Workplace (Health, Safety and
    Welfare) Regulations 1992, 102
Workplace (Health, Safety and
    Welfare) Regulations 1992., 102
Written statement of reasons for
    dismissal, 151
Written terms of a contract, 33